Betrayal of Trust

Betrayal
OF TRUST:
Sex and Power in Professional Relationships

JOEL FRIEDMAN *and*
MARCIA MOBILIA BOUMIL

PRAEGER

Westport, Connecticut
London

Library of Congress Cataloging-in-Publication Data

Friedman, Joel.
   Betrayal of trust : sex and power in professional relationships /
Joel Friedman and Marcia Mobilia Boumil.
      p.   cm.
   Includes bibliographical references and index.
   ISBN 0–275–95029–8 (alk. paper)
   1. Sexual abuse victims—United States.   2. Sexually abused
patients—United States.   3. Professional employees—United States—
Sexual behavior.   4. Professional ethics—United States.   5. Sexual
ethics—United States.   I. Boumil, Marcia Mobilia.   II. Title.
HV6592.F75   1995
362.88'3'0973—dc20   94–28004

British Library Cataloguing in Publication Data is available.

Library of Congress Catalog Card Number: 94–28004
ISBN: 0–275–95029–8

First published in 1995

Praeger Publishers, 88 Post Road West, Westport, CT 06881
An imprint of Greenwood Publishing Group, Inc.

Printed in the United States of America

∞
   The paper used in this book complies with the
Permanent Paper Standard issued by the National
Information Standards Organization (Z39.48–1984).

10 9 8 7 6 5 4 3 2 1

Contents

Preface

For decades people have put themselves in the hands of professionals, doctors, lawyers, clergy, educators, or others, with an unequivocal faith and trust that would not allow them to question even the competence, and certainly not the ethics, of their practices. They rarely questioned the advice; they did what they were told, and they were grateful for the privilege of doing so. Indeed, the professions were cloaked with a dignity and respect only deserved by and accorded to those of high honor and unquestionable character.

Today the realities are different. Each week the newspapers report the alleged wrongdoing of another trusted professional. Television shows regularly document these abuses and so today we have come to expect, and even demand, information, answers, and choices from the professionals who serve us. We routinely avail ourselves of second opinions in order to be sure that we can trust what we are told. Informed consent has become an expectation and not just an ideal.

Those of us who engage professionals are also quick to hold them accountable when something goes awry. Our despair over a poor result is as often voiced in the courts as it is in the privacy of our homes. And all too often, we are justified.

That, however, is not the end of the story. We have also come to recognize that the same professionals whom, only a short time ago, we thought we could entrust with our bodies and our souls, we now know may be capable not only of error or neglect, but also of intentional wrongdoing. Some have purposefully taken advantage of our naive trust, and that trust has been betrayed. And what is worse is that we were probably aware a generation ago of these same types of violations and were afraid to speak out.

Violations of trust by professional providers can occur in a number of ways. One of the most obvious is when they too often recommend services that are not in our best interests. Instead such services may yield an economic advantage to them, or perhaps an opportunity to experiment with our bodies at our expense. But a violation with even more serious consequences to the individual is the one that this book addresses: sexual exploitation. This occurs when a trusted professional uses his powers of persuasion and position to coerce an unsuspecting victim into sexual activity with him. Whether a victim consents because she is frightened of his power or persuaded by his supposed virtue, it is a clear professional violation and betrayal of our trust.

A generation ago the victims of sexual exploitation, mostly women, were usually afraid to speak out. And when they did, few people listened. But today the social climate has changed and women are willing, indeed encouraged, to stand up for their rights, speak out when they are violated, and pursue remedies against their abusers. This book is intended to inform, support, and encourage that end: to help victims anticipate and identify abusive situations, to promote awareness of their rights and recourse, and to assist them with the personal growth that can accompany their recovery from a betrayal of trust.

Joel Friedman
Marcia Mobilia Boumil

Introduction

It is currently estimated that one-third of all money awarded for medical malpractice is for damages for sexual misconduct. Indeed, sexual exploitation by professionals (defined as sexual contact with a trusted professional: doctor, lawyer, teacher, clergyman, or other, who is engaged to provide professional services) has come to be recognized as a problem of great magnitude in recent years. The sheer numbers of cases that have been reported, to say nothing of the vast majority which doubtless remain hidden, make it a problem of scandalous proportion.

Although both men and women can be victimized by professionals who are supposed to serve them, because of the dynamics of male/female relationships, as well as the usual hierarchy of greater status and position of men, the vast majority of victims are women. The great number of reported cases has made it possible to examine, ponder, and theorize about what makes so many women vulnerable to this kind of victimization. On the other hand, it has been much more difficult to understand what leads these men to jeopardize their status, power, and position and even their livelihood by engaging in sexually exploitative behavior.

Careful examination of the life stories, and specifically the underlying motivations, of both victims and perpetrators involved in a variety of sexual and other abusive relationships has led us to understand the fundamental aspects of male/female interactions that help set the stage for abusive or exploitative relationships when an opportunity arises. Of course, not all men take advantage of such opportunities, and presumably the great majority do not. But the interplay of what men and women look for in each other, what, in particular, attracts them to one another and how they express their attraction, gives insight into why "professional exploitation" is so prevalent. The following case of a bright, young corporate associate, whom we will call "Ginny," and her psychotherapist, whom we call Dr. Steven L., illustrates this point. As Ginny related to us first:

I was 27 years old and had gotten an M.B.A. from an Ivy League university 3 years earlier. I was working for a Fortune 500 company as a marketing analyst. The hours were long; the money was great and the people were terrific. Even my social life was as good as it had ever been. But still something wasn't right in my life. In fact, I had known for years that I suffered from a depression of sorts—one that I never quite understood. For years I had substituted studies and work and "community" service for a satisfying personal life. This job was perfect. I could completely immerse myself in my work, even doing extra things for the people around me, and nobody would ever know the difference, except me, when I arrived home each day to find my only stable companion—my cat.

After many years of avoiding this problem I knew it was time to come to terms with it and figure out what was going on with me. I came upon Dr. Steven L. quite by accident. His office was actually across the border in another state. I got him from a referral agency and my first priority was that my visits to him would be confidential.

Steve tells us that he distinctly remembers Ginny's first visit. He said:

- I recall that Ginny came into my practice at a difficult time in my life. The patient I saw just before her was a woman who always seemed to be angry and complaining and for whom no amount of work seemed to have any effect. After her I spent a few minutes on the phone with my wife trying to figure out where the money would come from to replace the roof and pay for our daughter's tuition. It was one of our typical brief but annoying interactions that usually left me cold. When Ginny came in I immediately noticed how young and sparkling she was. As she began to speak I found myself really paying attention to her. I was actually "present" in the session—completely, for the first time in a long time. She was particularly concerned that our sessions would be private and confidential and she accepted my assurance with an openness and naivete that were very refreshing.

Ginny recalls:

For me our first few meetings were uneventful. Dr. L. was a man of about fiftyish, tall, attractive, and well-groomed. He was polite in his manner and exceedingly patient. I noticed this particularly as time went on and we started getting into things that were really hard for me to talk about. He would keep me focused and he always seemed interested and attentive.

As Ginny tried to sort out her initial feelings of attraction to Steve, she commented:

There was something so comforting about just being there with a man who cared about what was going on with me. I was grateful for his willingness to listen to me, even if I had to pay for it. I was surprised at how close to him I began to feel and sometimes I would even ask him little personal things about himself. Usually he wouldn't respond directly, but one time I thought I could see him struggling—like maybe he wanted to tell me more. At some point during this time he asked me to call him "Steve." At first it was difficult but after a while it seemed quite natural. I realized how special it made me feel and how I began to have other feelings about him as well.

Steve continued:

I began to look forward to my sessions with Ginny. They were usually in the early evening, yet she always looked fresh and alert. She talked readily and often carried the sessions, making my work easier. When I offered an insight or a suggestion, she was always willing to consider it. She expressed gratitude for my help and she never failed to pay her bill on time. I felt recognized, youthful, and effective in my work with her. All this was happening and we hadn't even gotten into her story yet. I knew that I had great influence over this woman.

Ginny recalled:

After about a month we got into the subject of when my first prolonged feelings of sadness began and I ended up describing my parents' divorce. I was an only child and my father left when I was 11 years old. My mother was devastated and had so little emotional support to give me. In fact, most of the time she relied on my strength, even just to get up in the morning. She needed so much and I had so little to give.

Ginny related this sadly, as though taking care of her mother were somehow her responsibility.

I think it was during this discussion that the powerful reality of Steve as a man, probably as a father himself and as a "healer" overcame me. He, of course, would have understood how Mom and I felt. He, of course, would have thought about my needs. And he, of course, never would have left.

Steve also remembered this incident vividly:

As time went on and Ginny began to tell me some of the things that were going on with her I could sense her longing to be loved and cared for. Her parents had given her little and it was amazing how well she had met her own needs. She was not, however, hiding them from me and the more she shared the more important to her I felt. The rest of my life had become really routine, but my sessions with Ginny were different—they were alive. A couple of times I requested that she do little things for no particular reason—perhaps come earlier and wait in the waiting room or change her perfume. Whatever I asked, she just did it—without hesitation. I loved it.

When asked to describe her sexual attraction to Steve, Ginny recalls:

I can't quite describe it. First I saw him as the perfect father, and yet the quality in him that really captured me wasn't fatherlike at all: he seemed so smart, so worldly and so strong, and yet so sensitive and caring—the perfect mate.

Ginny described a particular meeting when her feelings for Steve reached a peak:

For weeks we had been talking about really important events in my life that I had never talked about to anyone. I discovered feelings that were deeply buried that I never even knew existed. Then one time Steve asked me about something so incredibly powerful for me that I just couldn't answer him. I opened my mouth, but nothing came out. So we just sat there, the two of us together, and the silence seemed to last forever. And through it all, all that I could think about was that I wanted him to touch me, hold me, and tell me that he'd never leave.

Steve recalled that session only too well:

Ginny was really very upset. She spoke slowly, tears gently flowing from her eyes, and then at one point she got tongue-tied and could only utter a helpless sigh. My mind raced ahead and as she spoke I found myself paying attention not to her words but to the smell of her scent, the sheen of her hair, and, of all things, the sexy turn of her ankle within the revealing sandal. I was overcome by desire, knowing I could have her whenever I wanted. This was the feeling I wanted to retrieve—what I thought I needed so I could feel whole again.

Ginny continued in a very deliberate tone:

When I finally looked up at him, it almost seemed like he, too, was mesmerized. I couldn't quite tell if he was unable to find the right words, or if he was just being patient, but he didn't say anything either. It was so hard to tell what was going on with him because of his calm manner, but at times it seemed like he really did care about me—as though somehow I really mattered. I couldn't take my eyes off him. For me there was so much "energy" in the room that I wished we could have made love right then and there.

In an instant Steve faced a defining moment in his life which he described this way:

> Our eyes remained locked and I knew Ginny was very vulnerable. I knew she would do whatever I asked of her. I also knew that I felt strong and whole again and that having her sexually would be wonderful for me. I even thought of how it would also allow Ginny to confront and work through her fears of abandonment. I reached across to her and began to gently wipe the tears from her face and my hands groped to feel the softness she willingly offered. I asked Ginny to come back that night after I had finished with my last patient. She eagerly agreed.

What you have just read is not a scene out of a romance novel; in fact, there is absolutely nothing romantic about it. It is not about love; it is really not even about sex. It is about power and exploitation. It is about what happens when an unethical professional encounters a psychologically vulnerable patient, client, student, or other and decides to use her trust in him, primarily engendered by his power and position, to his own advantage—with little regard to the consequences for her. It is about the nature of these professionals who deceive themselves and those who rely on them, and the contexts which provide fertile ground for this deception to occur. And this book is not just about psychotherapists—although the mental health professions provide the paradigm for professional exploitation. It is also about teachers, lawyers, doctors, and even the clergy who use their position to abuse those who come to trust them most. Our intention is not to titillate but to educate so that both potential victims and abusers alike will know how exploitation happens, why it happens, and what to do to prevent it. We will also provide some suggestions about how to remedy the damage that has already been done to thousands of unsuspecting victims.

Betrayal of Trust

Chapter 1

Sexual Intimacy in Professional Relationships

In recent years there has been an ever increasing awareness that various forms of sexual violence perpetrated primarily against women are occurring at an alarming rate. It is currently estimated that as many as one in three women is a victim of sexual abuse by a relative whom she knows and trusts. Rape is thought to occur somewhere in the United States every 30 seconds, more often than not committed by an offender who is known to the victim. Even sexual harassment is currently estimated to affect nearly 70 percent of American women, both in the school and on the job.

Today there is a growing awareness that there is yet another form of sexual violence, also primarily affecting women: sexual exploitation. Also sometimes referred to as "professional incest," sexual exploitation is perpetrated by professionals against the patients, clients, students, and others to whom they provide services. In the most common circumstance a female patient, client, or student seeks out the services of a professional man, and during the course of the professional relationship, he engages her in sexual activity. While, of course, the offenders are not always men nor are the victims always women, in most instances this is, in fact, the case. For the purposes of clarity this book will, therefore, generally refer to men and women, respectively, as perpetrators and victims of sexual exploitation.

Why, exactly, are sexual liaisons within professional relationships exploitative? There are two major ways in which women become victimized by these relationships. In the first, a victim is led to believe that this is an opportunity to share in an intimate relationship with a man whom, because of his power and position, she has come to respect, trust, and admire. Often he presents himself as a kind and caring professional, attentive to the needs of an unsuspecting female client, patient, or student and seeking to be helpful in whatever way his profession offers. At the same time, he is powerful and revered, a figure whose judgment one might otherwise never question. Often a victim becomes mesmerized by the thought that such an awesome person is interested, *really interested,* in her!

So what is wrong with that? In the great majority of cases, the intentions of the professional who approaches his clients, patients, students, and others in this manner are insincere. They are not based upon genuine interest in the individual; they are based upon the man's desire to use the relationship for his own sexual gratification: in short, to "exploit" her. And that's what's wrong.

> Lynne was approached by Dr. S., her gynecologist, whom she saw regularly for various matters as they developed over the years. She admired his wisdom and professional position and appreciated his kind bedside manner. When Dr. S. indicated at one point that he had a personal interest in Lynne, she felt honored that such an important man would be interested in her. He quickly engaged her in a sexual relationship with him which lasted only a few months. After that, his interest seemed to evaporate and he terminated the relationship abruptly.

Because of the nature of the relationship, the professional is often able to know where and how victims are vulnerable and to use the knowledge gained through the professional relationship to manipulate a victim in a manner that takes advantage of those vulnerabilities. If he is successful, she may willingly consent to a sexual relationship with him, only to be used, abused, and "dumped" when his needs are gratified and he no longer wants her. Her needs are rarely considered except to the extent that they are used to manipulate her.

In the second situation, the professional may or may not purport to have a genuine interest in his victim, but instead uses the professional relationship to coerce her, often subtly, to participate in a relationship with him. In these cases, the victim "consents" to the relationship, but her consent stems from fear that the professional services will be terminated if she does not acquiesce to his sexual desire.

> Kerry was referred by a friend to Attorney Jacobs when her marriage fell apart. He had the reputation of getting great results and Kerry was desperately afraid of losing custody of her son. From the beginning, Jacobs was reassuring about her position and made her feel good about herself at a time when she was feeling lonely and rejected. Kerry found herself looking forward to their meetings and was even pleased when his subtle remarks flattered her. She was taken by surprise, however, when he made his first sexual advance toward her. A part of her was clearly attracted to him; another part was skeptical about why he showed such interest in her; and yet another part was afraid to rock the boat with him because so much was at stake.

In most cases the sexual relationship that results is short-lived; it lasts until the professional man gets what he wants from it or gets tired of it, and then it ends abruptly. The incidence of this form of professional misconduct is alarming, and the consequences to the victims are often tragic.

The reality of sexual exploitation as an increasing social problem has generated a number of difficult questions. Indeed, it has been widely debated whether the various professions should assume an active role in determining whether, and under what circumstances, their members may engage in sexual or other relationships with the individuals they serve. On one side of the equation are two adults who may desire a consensual sexual relationship with one another. The law views this as a fundamental right of privacy and is loath to interfere with people engaging in mutually agreeable conduct with one another (so long as it is neither illegal nor immoral). Indeed, the law strongly protects this constitutional provision that people have a right to freedom of association. Yet on the other side of the equation is the professions' recognition that their members, merely by virtue of their power and position, can exert undue influence over the individuals they serve. What appears to be a consensual relationship is so fraught with an inherent imbalance of power and opportunity for undue influence that it can cause patient, clients, and students seemingly voluntarily to consent to such relationships without knowing that they are actually being exploited. And when the relationship runs its course and the professional moves on to someone else, the effects on the exploited individual are often so devastating that the law and the professions themselves are finding it necessary to step in and take responsibility: in short, preventing unsuspecting individuals from becoming victims of this type of abuse.

The various professions have dealt with the problem of sexual exploitation in different ways. The mental health professions, by far, have been most aggressive as it has become evident that the prevalence of sexual exploitation is enormous in that field. Indeed, the high incidence and seriousness of the consequences have led to the coining of the phrase "therapist-patient sex syndrome," indicating the magnitude of the professions' concern about the problem. The reason that sexual exploitation is so significant in mental health is well understood. The mental health professional is engaged to analyze, understand, and influence the patient's psychological and emotional state. The therapist's work requires that he act so as to elicit and sustain a deep sense of trust from his patient. If he is successful, this results in her willingness to expose to him psychological weaknesses and points of vulnerability.

In working with a mental health professional patients are encouraged to discuss parts of their lives that include intimate thoughts and feelings not generally shared with other people. The very process of doing so is likely to stimulate feelings of intimacy toward the therapist, particularly if he acts (as he should) in a manner that is kind, caring, and attentive. This scenario sets up a clear and direct opportunity for the mental health professional, who is often dealing with emotionally needy patients, to use the information that he has gathered during the therapy to manipulate them through their vulnerabilities: if he believes that a victim is insecure, he can become the perfect father; if he believes that she has poor self-esteem, he can promote a better self-image. The feelings of intimacy and attraction, which have physical as well as emotional components, are encouraged to develop during the therapy. They are supposed to be used as part of the healing process. If, instead, they are used to establish a sexual relationship, whether or not the therapist has a malicious motive, the harm that can be caused is often devastating. This is sexual exploitation.

Gynecology is another profession in which there exists the opportunity for sexual exploitation. As with mental health professionals, women discuss highly intimate matters with their gynecologists. They may discuss sexual function and dysfunction. They may discuss their marriage or other intimate relationships. As part of a routine examination, the woman allows the gynecologist to touch and even manipulate her genital areas. Even when there is no intent of either party to "sexualize" the relationship, it is often the case that a woman feels an intimate connection to her gynecologist. As a result, he has a great opportunity, similar to the psychotherapist's, to take advantage of that intimacy to urge sexual contact.

While there are the similarities indicated between therapists and gynecologists, the analogy goes only so far. Indeed, there are also important differences. Gynecologists do not routinely treat individuals who are mentally or emotionally compromised, in a current state of upset, or otherwise particularly vulnerable to psychological manipulation. Moreover, gynecologists do not necessarily have the expertise to recognize when and how a particular patient can be exploited. Time constraints and short and infrequent contacts usually limit the chances of strong, intimate feelings that require time and exposure to develop and usually occur gradually. So while some of the same factors may give gynecologists some special access to their patients, they do not squarely fall within the mental health paradigm, as significant differences make the analogy imperfect.

In recent years the occurrence of sexual exploitation and its negative consequences have also been observed within the legal profession. The incidence and severity have been less well documented, but sexual exploitation by lawyers is now clearly recognized and the profession is taking measures to protect potential victims from being harmed. To date, at least eleven states have ethical provisions in their codes of conduct which, in most circumstances, prohibit lawyers from engaging in sexual conduct with clients whom they represent. In addition, the states of California and Oregon have recently adopted rules that forbid sexual contact between lawyers and clients, at least to the extent that such relationships impair the lawyer's ability to represent the client adequately. New York has a similar provision applicable only to divorce lawyers. In creating these rules, the California Bar Association specifically acknowledged that attorneys can seriously harm their clients by engaging in a sexual relationship with them while providing their legal services. A number of other states (Illinois, for example) appear to be moving in the same direction, although specific rules have not been created as this book goes to press.

There are two common circumstances that give rise to clients' becoming sexually involved with their lawyers. In one, the client is emotionally vulnerable, perhaps going through a divorce. She feels lonely and rejected and looks to the lawyer not only to handle the legal matter but to help her through this difficult time. Not unlike what she expects from a therapist, she wants someone to listen, to sympathize, and to solve the problem. A lawyer who successfully fills this role will doubtless gain her admiration and respect and may win her sexual interest if he is intent upon doing so.

In an alternative circumstance the client may or may not be emotionally vulnerable when she engages the services of a lawyer to represent her. But after the professional relationship begins, a predatory lawyer attempts to use his power and position to cajole or coerce sexual favors. The client may believe that her acquiescence is beneficial or necessary for her case to be handled competently. She may feel trapped, not realizing that the lawyer can be fired. She may rationalize that it's okay, that it has nothing to do with her legal problem, or that it is worth putting up with to have her case go well.

Once again the analogy between lawyers and therapists is imperfect. Like gynecologists, lawyers do not always deal with emotionally vulnerable clients. And even when they do, they also do not necessarily know how to manipulate that vulnerability. The opportunity for intimacy is less certain, particularly if the legal matter concerns a purely economic transaction like a business deal or real estate matter. In those cases in which the lawyer (e.g., the divorce lawyer) does play the role of emotional caretaker, however, the opportunity for exploitation is significantly increased.

Teaching is yet another profession which has recently been forced to acknowledge that sexual exploitation is a significant problem. In fact, numerous colleges and universities have recently adopted policies that forbid faculty members to engage in sexual relationships with students whom they teach or supervise in any capacity. Once again, if mental health is the paradigm, these two professions have both common threads and important differences. Students, in general, do not present themselves with the same emotional vulnerability that a patient of psychotherapy might. Nevertheless, their lack of maturity can be just as disarming. It is not unusual for students to idolize teachers, and to follow their lead, simply assuming that their motives are pure. In a very real sense, students look to teachers as they look to their parents, and they expect their well-being to be protected in the same way. It is largely on that basis that faculty members are precluded from engaging in sexual conduct with students.

Still other professions have explored the ramifications of sexual exploitation within their own ranks and considered the need for regulation. In each case, the mental health profession is likely to be used as the paradigm. Each time, as the analogy to such a different profession becomes more imperfect, the argument for regulation becomes less compelling. But despite the differences between the mental health professions and the others, in most cases the basic and fundamental ingredients are shared: a difference in power and stature within the relationship and a fiduciary expectation that the professional will act in the best interests of the individual who trusts his intentions.

What about the clergy (but *not* those who are engaged in pastoral or spiritual counseling, as they function much as therapists do)? A clergyman is looked up to as a symbol of the deity or salvation. Does this perception affect how a parishioner might react to a sexual advance? Does the expectation of the clergy's fiduciary obligation to do no wrong affect a judgment about whether, in fact, such an advance is appropriate? The reality is that yet another group of professionals, the clergy, has a significant ability to exert undue influence over those whom they serve, and under such circumstances the potential for exploitation is very real.

Finally, consider the remaining health professionals: doctors, dentists, chiropractors, and others. They do not necessarily deal with emotionally compromised individuals. They are not presenting themselves as a servant of God. And the individuals they serve are not usually impressionable youth. Again, as we move away from the mental health paradigm, the opportunity for exploitation is less obvious, but nonetheless still present. Many of the basic elements still exist, and a vulnerable individual can be hurt just as badly. But it is also true that mutual, meaningful, and enduring relationships can also develop out of these encounters, so it becomes more and more difficult to regulate behavior as the indicia of danger become less apparent.

The mental health professions have dealt with the problem of sexual exploitation in a clear and decisive manner. Psychiatrists, psychologists, and social workers each have their own codes of ethics which separately but distinctly condemn sexual contact between therapists and patients under all circumstances. During the course of the professional relationship the codes decree that it is absolutely unethical for any such mental health worker to suggest, agree to, or participate in sexual contact of any kind with a patient or client. Even after the professional relationship ends, there are many in the field who believe that a subsequent sexual relationship between therapist and patient would still be exploitative because of the "timeless" nature of the clinical relationship. In fact, there is presently an ongoing debate about whether therapists ever can ethically engage in sexual relations with their former patients. The nature of this controversy as it pertains to the mental health and other professions will be explored in Chapter 9.

Sexual exploitation within professional relationships sometimes has been referred to as "professional incest." Although it is not incestuous in any traditional sense, it is nevertheless a descriptive characterization for a number of reasons. First, the perpetrators are individuals in whom the victims have placed their trust. As in parent/child relationships, the professional may be like a parent in the eyes of a child: powerful and caring, worthy of trust, and certain to never betray that trust. Like a parent, the professional is viewed as more competent than they and endowed with the expectation that the superior knowledge and skill would be used in their best interest. Indeed, many of us have been taught that the doctor can do no wrong and we maintain this faith, never dreaming that a revered and respected professional could actually have feet of clay. Many people tend to stereotype professionals, equating education and status with character and goodwill, and may be blind to the reality that professionals have human frailties.

> When Kerry's chiropractor began to touch her in a sexual way while purporting to treat her back problem, she assumed that it was part of the treatment. When his sexual advances became more obvious, she had a sense that a man who was engaged to perform this type of service should not be acting in this way, particularly during treatment. However, she knew him to be a "doctor" and trusted that he would not behave inappropriately during an office visit.

Another reason that sexual exploitation by professionals resembles incest is that the consequences to victims are remarkably similar to the effects observed in incest survivors. Women who are abused by someone whom they know and trust demonstrate distinct symptoms which usually are not present in victims of violence who did not know the offenders. They usually view their own participation as voluntary and therefore are likely to experience feelings of shame and guilt about having consented to the sexual conduct. They may feel anger at the perpetrator, but the anger is also turned inward to themselves, often leading to self-doubt and depression. As a result, they frequently demonstrate severely lowered self-esteem, social isolation, and sometimes self-destructive behavior, including suicide.

> Michelle was sexually exploited by her divorce lawyer when she was going through her second divorce. At the time she was emotionally distraught and he was very supportive, attending not only to her case but also her well-being. After she exposed the exploitation, many of her family and friends, although kind to her, treated her as though it was simply another affair that she agreed to out of poor judgment. In fact, she had demonstrated less-than-ideal judgment in the past, but this was not such a case.

What about the responsibility of the client, patient, or student who willingly consents to the sexual relationship with a professional whom she engages, perhaps even initiating it? The professions consider sexual misconduct involving a patient, client, or student to be the responsibility of the professional—regardless of whether or not he actually initiated the sexual behavior, or whether there exists an appearance of consent. This is because "true" consent is thought not to exist. What appears disguised as consent is too often impaired judgment resulting from ignorance, deception, or psychological manipulation of the client, patient, or student's vulnerabilities. Judy's experience illustrates this point.

> Judy sought the help of a psychologist after many years of suffering from recurrent episodes of depression. She was a single mother of twin girls and held a full-time job to support them. She was herself an only child with few family ties. After just a few sessions, Judy started looking forward to her sessions and to sharing her life with Dr. T., who was the only person who she felt could understand the stresses of single parenthood. Two months into the therapy, Judy had become quite attached to Dr. T., and he professed a strong attraction toward her. He told her that although he was a married man, he was actually quite lonely and would really enjoy a sexual relationship with her. Judy had become so dependent upon Dr. T. that being "special" to him was an opportunity that she felt she couldn't pass up. She knew, of course, that a sexual relationship with a married man was improper and was unlikely ever to

amount to anything, but it felt right for her at the time, and it gave her temporary relief from the depression which had plagued her for so long.

The statistics indicating the incidence of sexual exploitation by professionals are still being compiled. Data from the mental health professions indicate that as many as 10 to 12 percent of male therapists sexually exploit patients at some point in their career. Many do it often and repeatedly. Of those patients who are abused in this way, as many as 90 percent suffer serious consequences. Statistics on the incidence of sexual exploitation in other professions are still being gathered. In Massachusetts, for example, one researcher found that one-third of the money paid out in medical malpractice lawsuits was to compensate patients for injuries due to sexual misconduct by doctors. Both the justice system and the professions themselves are alarmed by the severity of this problem. "Conspiracies of silence" and the protectionism of "old boy networks" are giving way to efforts at finding solutions that both protect victims and preserve the dignity of the professions.

Chapter 2

Sexual Exploitation in the Mental Health Professions: The Paradigm

CASE STUDY: KRISTEN

It's been nearly 2 years since my relationship with Carl ended. He was a therapist that I went to see when my marriage to my second husband was in trouble. I was 31 and about to get divorced again. Everybody tried to tell me that it wasn't my fault—but I knew that I was responsible for a lot of it. Carl, Dr. M, that is, was recommended to me by another woman at work, who thought he was just great with relationship problems and self-esteem, and I thought that was just what I needed. I still had some hope of working out the trouble with Dan, my second husband, and this therapist sounded great.

It's hard to remember exactly how I felt about him in the beginning. He was an attractive man in his mid-forties, soft-spoken and incredibly sure about himself. I think that's what I liked most. He obviously felt good about himself and I was sure he could teach me to feel the same about myself. At first I saw him once a week, but after just a few weeks it was like I couldn't make it through unless I saw him, so I started making up excuses to need appointments more often. It's hard to de-

scribe what it was about him that was so alluring. As I look back I think
it was just that he was willing to listen to me. For the first time in my
life, someone would actually let me talk—and sit there, patiently, and
listen to me. I grew up in a large, overburdened family. My parents
didn't have much to give by the time I came along, and if I just wanted
to get heard, I had to be quicker and louder than everyone else. And
here was this man—he would let me take as long as I needed and he
would still be there, listening. At the beginning I mostly talked about
Dan. I talked a lot about being hurt, but I also tried to talk about how
deeply I cared about Dan. But if I ever thought this man was going to
help me keep my marriage together, I was dreaming. He had his own
agenda, and as I look back at it, it was there from the beginning. Every
time I would talk about maybe trying to work things out with Dan, he
would tell me that I deserved better and that I needed to "move on"
with my life. Sometimes I would end up feeling worse, but somehow
before I left I would always feel like I had to come back—like it would
be just another failure if I couldn't even be a good patient. Besides, I so
much wanted Carl to like me.

The hardest part of this story is to tell you how I felt about Carl. I
know I felt a very strong connection to him, probably because I got to
tell him about things that nobody else ever cared enough to hear about,
even the men I was married to. Dan really was a good man, and I think
that if we could have gotten him to come to therapy, there would have
been a real chance to work things out. Carl never even suggested it.
Instead it always seemed that in order to be a good patient, I had to
"move on," which meant away from Dan. I really wanted to work things
out, but Dan was angry and didn't make it easy for me to question
Carl's advice. Carl, on the other hand, showed me that men could be
kind and gentle and still be strong. What I realize now is that Carl
actually taught me that men can be kind and gentle if that's what they
think it takes to get what they want.

I had been seeing Carl for several months, starting once a week, but
scheduling more sessions when I wanted to see him or if I was really
upset, when his approach seemed to change. Instead of letting me talk
about whatever was on my mind, he started being more active and direct, asking me about how I felt about how things were going, and about
him. He began to make really explicit comments about me—my dress,
my hair, my makeup, and even my body—and also discussed some
things about himself. I was so hungry for attention that I just soaked it

up and went back for more. I felt special to Carl and looked forward to seeing him. Then one day it just happened.

I called him on a Monday morning to report that Dan had been very nasty to me and had decided to move out. I asked if he could squeeze in an "emergency" appointment. He was very accommodating and suggested that I come by at the end of the day since he had no other free time. When I arrived he seemed to be anticipating my arrival and greeted me warmly. I can remember how sweet he smelled as though he had just freshly showered. At the time I didn't think it was strange because I was consumed by what was going on in my life. He started by saying that he was glad that I could "reach out" to him in a crisis. I wasn't there for even 5 minutes when I fell apart and started to cry. Dan had left and I needed someone to care. Carl came over to me, put both arms around me, and led me over to his couch. For several minutes he just held me, but I couldn't stop crying. Then the next thing I knew, he was stroking my shoulders and as I relaxed he began to caress my breasts, making me feel wonderfully warm and safe. The contrast between how cruel Dan had been and how this man was treating me was stark and overwhelming. I was swept away.

When I stopped crying Carl talked to me in a voice that went right through me. He said that I was feeling rejected and lonely and that he knew what I needed. His touch, his calm and controlled manner, and his seemingly deep concern about me were what I felt I needed. There was no question in my mind that he knew what was right, and it seemed so fortuitous that he would be there and willing to give it to me. I was feeling like a carefree child, almost as though in a trance, and Carl seemed strong, caring, and protective. When he started to undress me I offered no resistance. I did whatever he told me to do, gave him what he wanted, and felt grateful to be able to repay his kindness.

For the next five-and-one-half months Carl would schedule end-of-the-day appointments for me twice a week. After about a month, things began to change once again. He would barely take the time to greet me before he would start getting undressed. His softness disappeared. He paid much less attention to my needs. After sex he would no longer talk about how special I was to him, but instead would tell me why sex with him was good for me and that it was part of my treatment. He continued to bill me at his regular hourly rate.

Between sessions, when I wasn't with Carl my feelings for him and what was going on were not always positive. On the one hand, I would say to myself, "Why not?" He was willing and nice and being with him seemed to improve the way I felt about myself. On the other hand, the "talking therapy" part of this relationship effectively stopped. Instead of my talking about what was going on with me, we would have sex and only talk about why it was so therapeutic for me. Sometimes it seemed wildly exciting; at other times it seemed cold and mechanical. It's difficult to explain, but a part of me felt safe and valued and another part felt like I was being used. The more confused I was the more attached to Carl I got. This was my escape from loneliness and another failed relationship. I was afraid to say "no." I was afraid to stop. I was pretty sure that if I didn't agree to sex, that would be the end of our relationship, and I wasn't strong enough to give that up. Ultimately it wasn't my choice.

As abruptly as this relationship began, it ended. One day Carl simply announced that his wife was complaining that he was getting home too late and he no longer had time for this aspect of my therapy, which he felt I no longer needed since I was "cured." I left obediently and became very, very depressed.

My ability to function was instantly disrupted. I spent the next three months in my apartment, mostly in bed. I couldn't go to work and eventually lost my job. I can't quite describe the level of my despair, but, basically, I didn't see any reason to go on living. This was worse than my divorce. I felt completely rejected and couldn't imagine ever being interested in anything again. Fortunately my best friend, Sarah, stood by me through all of it. She brought me food, talked to me, and literally kept me alive. She was the only person I trusted and eventually she succeeded in convincing me to get help. I was very scared and reluctant, but I couldn't stand the pain anymore. With Sarah's help I finally sought out another therapist—a woman this time. In the beginning I avoided any mention of my relationship with Carl, but she kept gently inquiring and eventually it spilled out.

My new therapist never pushed me but her encouragement helped me to talk about my experience with Carl. She was patient, accepting, and didn't try to talk me out of my feelings. She also explained the way therapy works, especially how it is normal to develop a strong emotional attachment to someone (particularly a therapist) who is kind, caring, and attentive. She also explained how an unethical therapist can exploit these vulnerabilities to satisfy his own needs. My new therapist helped me sort out what I did with Carl, and I came to realize that I was not to blame for what happened. Sometimes I still question whether I can trust anyone but I am feeling more confident and hopeful that I can also work through my failed marriages and problems with men and even start again in a new relationship.

WHAT ARE BOUNDARIES?

In every relationship, personal or professional, there necessarily exist certain physical and psychological "boundaries." The boundaries help define the relationship: in personal relationships people tend to get closer to one another, perhaps to touch each other in physical ways; they also tend to reveal more of their thoughts and feelings to each other. In professional relationships the boundaries are different: people generally keep a greater distance, both physical and psychological. Boundaries are important in relationships, not only because they establish the type of relationship, but because they also establish such points as where one's own reality ends and where another's begins. In fact, they distinguish one person from another, giving each a separate identity: this is me and this is you.

Unlike a physical boundary, which is tangible and often measurable, a psychological boundary is more abstract; it is made up of thoughts, feelings, sensations, and intuitions. But psychological boundaries, while intangible, are nevertheless very real. People with healthy boundaries are keenly aware of where their own "space" ends and where another's begins and can readily discern when a boundary has been crossed.

People without a healthy sense of boundaries, on the other hand, find it difficult to make those kinds of assessments. Sometimes it's even difficult to tell such things as what they themselves think, how they feel, and what they want: in short, how to define one's "self." Individuals without clearly defined boundaries may have a hard time distinguishing between their own needs and wishes and those of others. They may not be able to make decisions, know how they feel or what to think, and depend upon other people to tell them how to conduct themselves. The other's thoughts and wishes become the referent from which they make their own choices. So, instead of asking, "How do I feel?" "What do I think?" or "What do I want?" a person without strong boundaries will ask, "How does he/she feel?" or "What would he/she want me to do?"

The absence of a clear experience of boundaries makes it difficult to establish healthy or mature relationships with others. Without boundaries it is difficult to maintain a sense of limits: what is appropriate within the relationship and what is not. The absence of defined boundaries makes it dangerous even to have relationships because such people may not realize when a line is being crossed and their boundaries are being violated: a clear indication that the relationship may be dangerous or abusive. Indeed, for just this reason people without healthy, defining boundaries tend to enter and stay in harmful or exploitative relationships.

Psychological boundaries are largely put into place during childhood. The child's experience (how it is treated by family and other important people) determines how its boundaries become defined and how well they will subsequently function. When a young child's needs are met (e.g., it receives appropriate responses, is properly fed and clothed, and is made to feel safe and secure), the child develops a sense of personal boundary. This is because when it is hungry, tired, otherwise uncomfortable, and cries to be cared for, it gets attention. The child learns what its own experience is; what it senses and feels, and eventually what it thinks. These experiences belong to the child, and together they form a sense of a "self" delineated by boundaries. The child may test the limits of its boundaries by crying louder, longer, or more frequently, and it learns how far its personal boundary extends.

When a child's needs are not met (because they conflict with those of its caretakers), the child's boundaries become defined by the needs of others, limiting the development of the sense of "self." The child does not learn to experience its own needs; it experiences only the needs of others. This blurs the boundaries between the child and others, ultimately preventing the child from differentiating its own needs from those of others.

As a young child, Katie was praised and rewarded by her mother for physical closeness (hugs, etc.) and proximity (keeping Mom company rather than playing with peers). She was also rewarded for adopting her mother's interests and attitudes, which her mother considered a sign of respect. In fact, Katie's mother felt threatened by signs of her independence, fearing that it would result in Katie's growing up and leaving her. As an adult, Katie had a confused sense of who she was (her emotional boundary). In her relationships she sought consensus and withdrew from conflict. She sought to please others and felt valued and comfortable when she was able to do so.

Peter grew up as an only boy in a family with four siblings. When Peter was a young child, his father wanted him to achieve everything he had wanted for himself: to be an athlete, a professional man, financially successful, etc. When Peter was frightened to try something new, his father would push him to succeed. At times Peter would rebel and withdraw, particularly when his lack of ability disappointed his father. As an adult, Peter also had a distorted sense of emotional boundary. He was afraid to get too close to people, fearing that his inadequacy would ultimately lead to rejection.

Early experiences are important in determining the strength of an individual's boundaries: when they are secure, where they are weak, and how they can be breached. Young children, still undeveloped, are particularly vulnerable, and all children as they are in the process of developing are at risk for having their emotional "space" invaded at times. Greater violations, such as violent acts of assault or trauma, and an extended duration of violation, such as sexual or emotional abuse over a period of months or years, have significant enduring effects on the child's development of boundaries.

Tammy's parents believed that physical illness and out-of-sorts behavior were the result of contaminants in the body being stored up in the colon and bowels. Whenever Tammy wasn't feeling well or misbehaved, they would give her an enema in order to "detoxify" her, getting rid of the poisons in her body. She would cry, scream, and beg them not to hurt her, but she was made helpless as a result of being restrained while her body was violently entered. Tammy had no control of either her physical or psychological boundaries.

Psychological boundaries can also be violated through deceit and manipulation.

When Jill was 4 years old she attended nursery school. She developed a strong attachment to the class pet, which was a long-haired guinea pig named Sally. She really loved this animal and fed and attended to it as though it were her own. During school vacation she was asked to take Sally home and care for her. Jill was delighted. Although she knew that she would be away for part of the vacation, she was sure that her father would care for Sally in her absence. While she was away, her father neglected Sally and she died. Before Jill returned, her father decided to replace Sally, only to find that hers was a rare breed. Instead he replaced it with a short-haired breed which also had different facial markings. When Jill returned, her father told her that he had given Sally a haircut. Jill burst into tears, insisting that it wasn't Sally, but was admonished to control herself. Her father didn't want to hear any more about Sally. It wasn't until many years later when her grandmother died while Jill was away at college and she was never informed until the end of the semester (so she wouldn't ask to travel home) that she realized that this was a lifelong pattern of deception, of which Sally's disappearance was the first remembered incident.

EXAMPLES OF DAMAGED BOUNDARIES

The following are some examples of how damaged boundaries are often experienced by the individual. This is not an exhaustive list, but it indicates many of the telltale signs of weakened or vulnerable boundaries that put a person at risk for being manipulated. These are:

- It is difficult for you to ask for what you want and need and hard to say "no" to other people when you would like to.
- It is easier to take care of other peoples' needs and desires than your own. It is also easier to go along with them than express your own opinions.
- Other people seem to know you better than you know yourself. They also seem to know what is best for you.
- It is hard to make decisions because you frequently don't know how you feel or what you think about important things.
- When feelings are present they are so strong that they are overwhelming. It is difficult to control the "volume," to turn feelings up or down and still be in touch with them.
- Relationships seem to be one-way and you always put more into them than you get out of them. But even though you're not getting what you want, you stay with them just the same.
- Other people's moods have a big effect on you because you feel responsible for them. When they are happy, you are happy. When they are sad or angry, you blame yourself.

Chapter 3

Sex and Power in Other Professional Relationships

CASE STUDY: DEBBIE

I was referred to Dr. F., a highly regarded obstetrician/gynecologist, by a girlfriend who had just delivered twins through natural childbirth. It was at a time that natural deliveries were just beginning to come into vogue in this country and few physicians were willing to do them yet. I was not pregnant at the time but my husband and I wanted children and I thought that when the time came, I, too, would love to try this new approach to childbirth.

When I first met Dr. F. I remember being taken aback by him. He was a strikingly handsome man with a manner that was so gentle and sophisticated that any woman would have to be attracted to him. But as I came to know him better, it was clearly more than his looks and his manner that swept me off my feet; it was his patience with me and his willingness to talk as much as I needed to about my concerns about birth control, getting pregnant, and even starting a family. When he fitted me with a diaphragm, for example, I had a hard time manipulating it. Dr. F. was a very patient teacher and he would help me practice until I felt more capable of doing it correctly and quickly.

One time when I went to see Dr. F. I was still having trouble with

the diaphragm and he asked me if something was going on with Joe that
was affecting my use of contraception. I just couldn't get the hang of it
and he figured, rightly, that maybe something was wrong in my marriage. Well, I never would have even mentioned it to anyone else, but I
was really starting to resent the fact that I had to use contraception
because Joe was still not "ready" to start a family. We had been married
for 6 years and I wasn't getting any younger, but Joe kept putting me
off and there never seemed to be a "good" time to talk about having a
child. Dr. F.'s interest and patience were very supportive to me and I
felt grateful to him.

After about 6 months that subject became obsolete when, inadver-
tently, I ended up getting pregnant anyway. Joe actually surprised me
by being uncharacteristically loving, and before the baby was born, I
think he actually got excited about the prospect of fatherhood. Even
Joe's renewed sense of commitment to me, though, didn't seem to affect
my growing attachment to Dr. F.

My first pelvic examination after I got pregnant was something I will
never forget. Instead of doing the usual Pap smear and internal exam,
Dr. F. had me lie on his table and went about touching and examining
my entire body. His hands glided so easily that it was as though he were
giving me a massage, and for the first time in my life it felt as though I
were being touched by a man who really cared about me. And then, as
though it were planned that way, he hooked up the machine that let me
hear my baby's heartbeat for the first time, and he was there to share
one of the most wonderful moments of my life.

As delivery grew near, my apprehensions about motherhood started
to set in. What if I don't know how to care for a baby? And what if.
. . . Dr. F. was always there to answer my questions and quell all of
my fears. What a perfect human being, I thought, and, of course, Joe
paled by comparison. What I didn't realize was that Dr. F. was setting
me up for a ride, and that it would end with me flat on my face. Somehow by telling my story, I hope that it won't happen to someone else.

Near the end of my pregnancy I was feeling awkward and unattrac-
tive, weighing more than I had ever weighed at any other time in my
life. Joe wouldn't even approach me sexually, supposedly because he
didn't want to hurt the baby. But I felt fat and clumsy and got suspicious
every time Joe even looked at another woman (who, of course, always
seemed graceful by comparison). I even started to wonder whether
something was going on between Joe and our housekeeper. Dr. F., on
the other hand, always commented on my appearance, saying things like

Chapter 4

Early Warning Signs: The Prelude to Exploitation

CASE STUDY: CAITLIN

I was a sophomore at a small college in Minnesota. All of my life I wanted to be an engineer. My parents tried to convince me to be a nurse or a schoolteacher, but I was determined not to get stuck in women's jobs. I grew up as the only girl in the shadow of two successful brothers, and I wanted to accomplish something myself. I was tired of not being taken seriously because, after all, I was just a *girl.*

I made it through my freshman year without too much trouble, even though I felt very isolated because there were only two other women in my program. The next year, though, was different: I had to take the physics courses. I hated physics. There was just something about it; I never seemed to be able to make sense of that subject. Right from the beginning I dreaded the course, but I knew I had to get through it.

Jack T. was a part-time professor who just came in to teach beginning physics. You could tell from the start that he was different from a lot of other professors. He really *was* an engineer, and he worked in the field at a high-level job. He didn't just sit around the school and teach theory; he was out there doing important things and making a name for himself.

Even though I hated physics, I had a sense that I could relate to Jack (which, by the way, he wanted us to call him). He was down-to-earth, and he knew his stuff. You could see that he lived in the real world, and he always made a point of showing us how a theory would be applied in a real situation. It's hard to explain, but after a few weeks I wasn't so scared about physics anymore. The subject matter still daunted me, but I felt okay in the course—like somehow I would make it through.

Three weeks after the course started, Jack posted his office hours. Since most of the time he was not around, it wasn't as though you could casually drop in. You had to make an appointment and when he said he was available, I was first to sign up. I actually wasn't having a particular problem at the time, but I was still so afraid of physics that I thought I'd better get some help anyway.

Our meeting was scheduled right before class, and when I got there Jack was so nice that I couldn't believe it. We talked about engineering; we talked about me; we talked about the college; we even talked about my parents. Everything seemed so easy. We never even mentioned the course; we spent all of the time just getting to know each other. When the hour was over we ended up walking back to class together, and just before I sat down he invited me to come back next week to talk about whatever I had come for, since we never even got around to that. I agreed impulsively and the next week couldn't come fast enough.

There were so many things that passed through my mind over the next few days that I don't think that I even fully appreciated what was going on. It was hard being in a program with so few other women. It was hard being away from home. Even though I was never very popular in high school, I always had a small group of close friends, and when something came up, there was always someone to talk to. Boy, did I wish they were around now to talk about Jack.

When I returned for my next meeting the following week, Jack was again as nice as could be. He really seemed to care about me. It's funny, but in class he was always so focused on the material that you'd never know how nice he really was. Alone he was very different, and I felt that I could talk to him about anything. This time we did get around to the purpose of my visit. I told him that although I wasn't completely lost yet, I knew it would only be a matter of time since physics was so hard for me. He seemed to immediately understand, and offered to set aside a regular hour for me—a "tutoring" session, of sorts. That was just fine with me, and the thought of saying "no" never even crossed my mind. I felt like I had been saved.

Chapter 5

Filing a Complaint Against Your Therapist: The Mental Health Paradigm Revisited

CASE STUDY: ABBY

It's been 4 years since my relationship with Jerry ended. He was a therapist whom I went to see because I was having a hard time after my divorce and trouble with my 7-year-old son, Joey. I was still very angry at my ex-husband, Steve, who left me to marry his 22-year-old secretary. Every time Joey would spend a weekend with Steve, he would come back and talk all about his dad's fiancée and how he would be lucky to have two "moms" after the wedding. It was driving me crazy and my best friend, Donna, recommended that I talk to her therapist. I was skeptical at first, because I never thought that he would be able to do anything. But Donna raved about him so much that I thought I would give it a try.

Within a couple of sessions he had told me everything I wanted to hear: that I wasn't crazy; that I had the right to be mad at Steve; and that I was a special person and had a lot going for me. Sometimes he would just stare at me and tell me how pretty I looked and how a man would be "nuts" to let go of me. After a few weeks I knew I was really getting attached to this man. I'm not really sure why, but he was so caring and attentive and I really got to love just being with him. I guess he knew what I needed and he knew just what to say.

And then it just happened. I showed up one day for a session and we ended up making love. It seemed so easy, so natural, and so right. We were both lonely, both searching for someone else—and both perfect for each other. Or so I thought. Our relationship lasted for about five-and-one-half months. We would see each other every week at my regular appointment and sometimes in between. We would talk about ourselves and each other and what we wanted out of life. And mostly we had sex. A couple of times he was so eager to get my clothes off that it seemed like that's all he really wanted. But I kept telling myself that Jerry really cared about me and that's just how he showed it.

The relationship ended much the same way that my marriage ended: one day Jerry just dumped me. He said that he had to "scale down" his practice and he no longer had time to see patients who didn't really need him. He said that I was fine and he even hinted that the sex I had with him was just what I needed to help me and that I was "cured" now. This man who had been so kind and so caring just all of a sudden didn't need me anymore.

What was different about being dumped this time was that I had become attached to Dr. Jerry in a way that I had never felt with Steve. It seemed like I could talk to him about anything, and he was never critical or demeaning. At times it seemed like he understood me even better than I understood myself. It seemed so perfect. When it ended I was devastated. I was so upset and I didn't have anyone to turn to. I couldn't even tell Donna because I had never told her what had gone on between me and Dr. Jerry and I just couldn't tell her now. This time I was really depressed, and not because of Steve and Joey, but because of what happened with this man who, only 6 months earlier, didn't even exist in my life. I had forgotten all about my ex-husband of almost 10 years and the father of my child, and I was devastated by a man I barely knew. It made no sense. It seemed that he knew exactly what he was doing. I was in love, or so I thought, and I didn't pay much attention to anything else. He was billing my insurance company for the time that we were having sex.

Almost 2 years after this happened, Donna confided in me something that I could never have told her: Jerry had been having sex with her. And at about the same time he dumped me, he dumped her also. She was as torn up inside as I was and for weeks we would talk about nothing else. We found strength in each other and sometimes we would fantasize about getting revenge. Then one day just as our rage was starting to subside, Donna read something in a magazine about sex between therapists and patients being unethical and possibly illegal. She followed up this article and we both began to see how we were really abused and why this experience had been so especially painful for both of us. We became like two women looking for a cause and we were willing to do anything to get back at this man. Probably neither of us might have pursued him alone, but together we managed to get through a lot of embarrassment and a lot of legal red tape.

First we went to the State Board of Registration, where this man was licensed to practice. They took our complaint but told us they would have to begin an investigation and that because of funding cutbacks, the backlog for investigating complaints was quite long. After many weeks of waiting, we went back to follow it up and found that they had not yet even begun to process our papers. This went on for about five-and-one-half months and finally someone from the Board of Registration contacted us. It was a man who took our story again; he remarked that there were no other complaints on file about this therapist and he did not know exactly how far this investigation would go. Several months after that we were told that Dr. Gerald P. had been called before the Board and denied any wrongdoing. Because there were no other complaints on file, no formal disciplinary action was taken and the file was closed.

At about the same time that we were waiting for some action by the licensing board, Donna had also heard that some of these cases were being brought to court. She didn't know whether they were going through criminal channels or whether lawsuits could be brought, but after we heard the decision of the Board of Registration, we decided to see a lawyer.

Neither Donna nor I had any great familiarity with lawyers so I went to the woman who did my divorce. She was nice enough and seemed competent but she had never heard of patients' suing psychotherapists for improper sexual contact. When she looked into it, however, it was another story. She found that several states actually had criminal laws against therapist-patient sex and, if we had been in such a state, the therapist could actually go to jail. Our state did not, so we had to pursue him ourselves.

Our lawyer suggested the possibility of a civil lawsuit. She said that the therapist could be sued because his conduct was unethical and usually considered to be malpractice. In fact, she said that if he had malpractice insurance, it might even pay our claim. In any event our case was likely to get a lot of media attention and Jerry was certain to be embarrassed and humiliated, even if we ultimately lost our lawsuit.

That was the good part. What we also found out is that lawsuits are tough on both parties. We had to expect to be asked about the details of our sexual relationship with the therapist, as well as with anyone else. We had to expect the details of our therapy to be discussed (even though they were supposed to be confidential) since we were suing the therapist. And we had to expect that he would lie, probably deny ever having touched us, and probably suggest that we were hysterical or nuts or were even hallucinating the whole thing. Of course, we were lucky that there were two of us; otherwise there might be no one to back up our story.

In the unlikely event that Jerry admitted that he had sex with us, there would be another set of legal obstacles. He would undoubtedly claim that we consented—and, indeed, we did. He would probably say that we asked for it—and maybe we did. And then there was the time problem. The law doesn't let you wait forever before you have to bring your lawsuit, and we might have already waited too long.

After the lawyer explained all of the procedural pitfalls, then she got to the hardest part of all. She asked us whether we were prepared to see Jerry, face-to-face, and accuse him of luring us into a sexual relationship with him. She needed to know whether we could handle the cross-examination about the most intimate parts of our lives—whatever they asked us. We would undoubtedly be asked about why we ever consented, and whether we led him on. We had to expect that Jerry would use whatever he had learned about us to try to force us to drop our lawsuit. In many ways this seemed to be the ultimate violation, but, ironically, one of the few things that Jerry managed to teach us was to have the strength to go forward with what we believed. And so we did.

A victim who has been sexually exploited by a professional may have available several courses of action from which to choose, depending upon the state where the services were rendered and the nature of the recourse sought. In the mental health field (where there are established procedures) the various options include filing a complaint with the Board of Registration that licenses the therapist (if he is licensed), filing a complaint with a professional association or society (if any) of which the therapist is a member, filing a criminal complaint (in those eleven states that have a criminal law against sexual exploitation by therapists), and/or filing a civil lawsuit to collect monetary compensation from the offender. This chapter will set forth the criminal, disciplinary, and licensure penalties that a victim of sexual exploitation by a therapist may pursue; Chapter 6 addresses the possible civil options.

ADMINISTRATIVE REMEDIES

Professional Organizations

There are numerous professional associations of which a psychotherapist may be a member. On the national level such professional organizations include the American Psychiatric Association, the American Psychological Association, the National Association of Social Workers, the American Psychoanalytic Association, and the American Association for Marriage and Family Therapy. On the local level virtually every state has a similar association (e.g., the Massachusetts Psychological Association). Participation in these organizations is voluntary. A practitioner may be a member of all, some, or none of these organizations. Thus the first task for a victim who chooses the administrative route is to determine which, if any, have him as a member.

Once it is determined that the therapist does belong to one or more such organization(s), the next step is to file an "ethics" complaint. Victims can call the organization identified and inquire about the appropriate procedure, but typically there is a specific form (often provided by a subcommittee which initially investigates complaints of ethical violations) which can be sent out. The form will seek a detailed description about what happened and why the victim believes that it constitutes a violation of the association's ethical policies. In cases of sexual exploitation, the violation is usually clear. For example, the ethical code of the American Psychiatric Society specifically states the following:

> The necessary intensity of the therapeutic relationship may tend to activate sexual and other needs and fantasies on the part of both the patient and therapist, while weakening the objectivity necessary for control. Sexual activity with a patient is unethical.

It is important to keep in mind that in virtually all cases the complainant will be required to sign the complaint. Many victims would prefer to issue a complaint anonymously, even if they think that the therapist would know who complained. However, in the vast majority of cases the process will not go forward unless the victim is willing to sign (and likely swear to) the charges and ultimately to defend them if necessary.

Some victims back out when they find that it's necessary to sign the complaint. Why? First, they find out that when they file a complaint, they have to sign a "waiver," which means that the therapist can go into their file and dig out whatever confidential information he has about them to use to defend himself. It doesn't mean that he can use personal information that doesn't have any bearing on the complaint, but a lot of victims are ashamed of or embarrassed about what might come out, and they're not willing to risk what might be said.

Another reason that victims back out is that they become frightened of retaliation from the therapist or publicity that makes it known that they were patients. In fact, actual retaliation is rare, and the maximum possible confidentiality is maintained. The reality is, however, that when a victim files a complaint, some of the privacy (the so-called privilege from disclosure) is lost and it is not always predictable what might be disclosed about the complainant.

The next step, if it is at all possible, is to identify or locate other victims. This is extremely important because a complaint with more than one victim is likely to be taken very seriously, which is not to say that a single complaint would not. But if two or more victims corroborate each other's story, a favorable outcome is likely. So how might a victim find other victims? One route is for the victim to talk to whoever made the referral to this therapist. If it is an individual, the victim might inquire about his or her experience, and that of others who were referred. If the victim referred other people, she might inquire about what their experience was. Particularly in smaller communities, often this type of news gets around, and often somebody knows somebody who had a similar experience. Also, since psychotherapy is a field in which word-of-mouth referrals are the norm, often a "network" of patients who are served by the same therapist is formed. And since an abusive therapist is likely to have more than one victim, there is some chance that others can be identified.

Another possibility for finding other victims is to inquire with the local licensing board or professional association that is handling the complaint. It may not reveal the identity of other victims, but usually it will tell a complainant whether or not other complaints have been filed. This information may be valuable for future use.

The next step is that the association will disclose the complaint to the accused therapist and require him to respond in writing. He has a certain period to do so, but often it will be extended and committees are generally quite liberal about allowing as much time as is needed. One possibility that the victim needs to be aware of at this point is that the therapist may file a "countercomplaint," which means that he attempts to accuse his accuser of some misbehavior. Since presumably the victim is not a member of that organization, a complaint against a nonmember doesn't have any "teeth"; actually its intent is to harass and intimidate the complainant. It also gives the victim some idea about whether the therapist is going to admit his wrongdoing or instead attempt to malign and discredit the victim. Even for a victim who knows that she is right, sometimes it takes a lot of strength to go forward. Many victims think it just isn't worth the effort.

After the accused therapist submits his written response, an investigation is usually started, unless it appears clear from the complaint that no ethical violation occurred or unless the conduct is admitted. Since there is no real "defense" to sexual misconduct, the circumstances of the matter do not really matter and a formal investigation will not be required. In most cases, however, the misconduct is at least initially denied and the committee handling it will investigate the matter. The victim is not usually involved in this phase unless the committee has to come to her for more information.

The next step in this proceeding is that a meeting is usually convened so that a hearing can be held. Sometimes, but not always, the accuser will be asked to be present. The most important factor that determines whether or not the victim is needed is whether there is a dispute with the therapist about what happened. If he admits to his conduct, the victim does not need to be there to hear it. Even if he attempts to accuse the victim of willingly participating and even encouraging it, it still should not matter. Sexual misconduct is always the responsibility of the therapist, and the fact that the victim agreed does not affect that obligation.

After the hearing, the subcommittee generally makes a recommendation to the entire ethics committee. Eventually it will be heard by the full Board of Directors. Their functions are to determine the final disposition of the case and to vote on a penalty. Penalties range from requiring a verbal or written apology to expelling the practitioner from the organization. Unfortunately, even expulsion cannot prevent a therapist from practicing, and usually the professional associations recommend less harsh penalties (except for repeat offenders) since once a therapist is expelled, no professional organization may be left to monitor his conduct. Many victims are discouraged from pursuing this course simply because the penalties aren't harsh enough. What they may not realize, however, is that the consequences to a therapist of disciplinary proceedings are much greater than can be measured by the penalty: sometimes it ruins his future ability to get clients or even to practice.

The complaint process from beginning to end can take anywhere from a few months to a couple of years. Many victims get frustrated by the delays, particularly if they think that the cause is that their complaint is not being taken seriously. Yet another frustration is that victims are not always advised of the disposition of their cases. Sometimes they hear nothing. If they inquire, however, they should at least find out whether the therapist was found to be guilty or not, even if the association will not tell what, if any, penalty was imposed.

And what, exactly, are the possible penalties? The most common ones include requiring the therapist to apologize, monitoring (through supervision) the therapist's work, putting the therapist on probation (as a member of the organization), and expelling him from the organization. In general, sexual misconduct is considered to be a severe offense and the more severe penalties would apply. In those cases where it is a first offense, however, particularly if only one victim comes forward, a lesser penalty might be expected.

The benefit of choosing this route is that there need not be any expense to the victim; it is not necessary to hire an attorney. In fact, the complainant may not even need to testify or confront the abusive therapist. On the other hand, there are also some drawbacks to this procedure. First, not all practitioners are members of professional organizations (and therefore bound by their ethical codes). If the therapist is not a member, the organization will not take the complaint. Second, many victims find the procedure for filing complaints with these organizations complicated. Others feel that the ethics procedure seems inherently unfair because the committee is itself made up of other psychotherapists who could be prejudiced on behalf of their colleagues. In the past, this was, in fact, often the case. It seemed futile to file a complaint because it would be processed by the "old boy network." The professionals seemed to protect their own, and complaints seemed to be "quashed," "misfiled," or otherwise trivialized.

Today this is usually not the case. With the increase in courageous victims coming forward and the extensive media coverage that some cases have received, the therapists themselves now understand the seriousness of the problem of patient-therapist sex and the damage it causes both to patients and to the profession. So today they are more likely to be both interested in and motivated toward putting a stop to the problem.

Victims still complain that resolutions are inadequate because the professional association's most potent remedy is mere expulsion from that organization. Of course, it is true that an abusive therapist is not prevented from practicing and, indeed, continuing to abuse other patients. Ethics complaints do make a difference, however. A therapist who is accused once must always look over his shoulder and wonder whether it might happen again. It tarnishes his professional reputation and standing in the community. More importantly, it may cause him to examine his own behavior seriously, and in the long run that may be the greatest benefit.

Licensing Authorities

If a victim thinks that a complaint to a professional organization is an inadequate remedy because of the narrow range of penalties, a complaint with a licensing board may provide a better solution. Licensing boards get their authority from state governments to oversee the practices of professionals who are licensed by them. They are also obligated to protect consumers by, among other things, revoking the licenses of professionals who are unfit to practice. Generally psychiatrists are under the licensing authority of the state medical board, while psychologists, social workers, and other counseling professionals are licensed, if at all, by separate professional licensing boards.

Just as the professional association may not be able to provide any recourse because the therapist is not a member, so licensing boards may also be unable to reach an abusive therapist. In many states, therapists need not be licensed to practice and can even practice if their license is revoked. For example, in most states a psychologist must hold a license in order to call himself a "psychologist" publicly, but no particular license, training, or experience is necessary to call or advertise himself as a "psychotherapist" or "counselor." As a result, when a patient is referred to such a person, she may not know unless she is willing to ask exactly what his credentials are or whether a complaint has ever been filed against him.

The complaint procedure with a licensing board is similar to that of a professional organization. The complainant fills out a written complaint identifying the name, dates, and specific acts of the accused. The licensing board can either forward the complaint to the state attorney general's

office, if the conduct reported is criminal in that state, or can process it
and begin its own internal investigation. After a preliminary investigation, the board may decide to file a formal complaint, or, if it decides
that the charge is without merit, to close the case.

Assuming that the case is found to have merit, the board has the
option of trying to settle the matter. This means that if the therapist
admits that the sexual contact occurred, he can voluntarily submit to the
recommendation of the board (e.g., censure, probation). If he does not
admit it, or if he and the board cannot agree on a sanction, it is then
usually submitted to an administrative law judge, who decides the matter. An administrative proceeding occurs without a jury and without the
same procedural rules that would apply in a court of law. However, the
accused therapist will usually have an attorney and evidence will be
presented as in any other case. A decision is rendered by the judge on
the basis of the evidence that is presented.

Usually in a licensure proceeding the accused will be called upon to
testify. Since the accused is a "witness," it is not necessary for her to
have a lawyer, but if she's thinking about a civil suit later on, she may
want to consult one before the hearing to advise her about what she
might say that would affect the subsequent civil suit. The accused can
also be "cross-examined," which means that both sides will ask questions, and once again the accused loses the privacy and confidentiality
that otherwise govern those sessions spent with the therapist. Fortunately
there are enough safeguards that truly confidential information should
not be revealed unless it is directly related to the sexual contact.

The decision of the administrative judge is sent back to the licensing
board, which is then entitled to accept or reject the decision. The action
of the licensing board is final, however, and if the therapist later attempts to go to court to challenge it, the decision will likely be upheld.
The boards have a number of sanctions available to them, including
suspension or revocation of a license, reprimand (e.g., public criticism),
censure (e.g., public or private disapproval), a fine, or even the require-
ment that the therapist perform a certain amount of public service.
Among the many cases that have been brought over the years, the full
range of various sanctions has been imposed.

Disciplinary proceedings conducted by licensing authorities also have
a number of advantages and disadvantages. The major advantage is that
the accused avoids going to court and testifying in an open forum, perhaps before a jury. Further, if the board finds against the therapist, the
cost to him can be great, including public embarrassment and loss of his

license to practice his profession. However, the cost to the accused is usually less than it would be if a court action were involved.

The disadvantages of an administrative proceeding are also significant. Although the accuser is spared going to court, she must usually appear at the administrative hearing. This can be very stressful, particularly for someone who has already been abused once. The complaint and proceedings can also be time-consuming. More importantly, however, the victim has to be prepared to discuss and repeat her story a number of times throughout the proceeding. And in the end, even if the most potent remedy, license revocation, is imposed, in many cases the offender can still practice, unlicensed, under a different title.

Gerri was devastated when her psychotherapist, who engaged her in a sexual relationship 2 months after she began therapy, decided that he no longer had time to continue that relationship. Gerri had not told anyone about it, but it came out when she became suicidal, and the therapist was reported to his licensing board. She had just started with a new psychotherapist and had not yet been able to confront this experience when the licensing board called her to testify. During the hearing she was asked, repeatedly and in painstaking detail, exactly what happened and how she participated. Throughout the hearing she felt as though she were on trial. When her new therapist tried to guide her in working through the experience to heal the wounds, Gerri simply could not go over it again, and this reluctance inhibited her recovery.

Criminal Complaints

Currently eleven states have criminal laws that make it illegal for a mental health professional to engage in a sexual relationship with a patient: California, Colorado, Florida, Georgia, New Hampshire, Iowa, Maine, Michigan, Minnesota, North Dakota, and Wisconsin. There are also some states that are considering similar legislation (Maryland, Massachusetts, New Mexico, and Pennsylvania). The purpose, of course, is to discourage sexual misconduct further by making it a criminal offense (indeed, often a felony) and increasing the penalties for those who are found guilty.

For the most part the criminal statutes, as drafted, are far-reaching. For example, the Wisconsin statute applies to all persons who practice or present themselves to the public as practicing as therapists, whether or not they are licensed. This includes psychiatrists, psychologists, social workers, nurses, counselors, and the clergy. It also covers a wide range of sexual "contact," including intercourse, oral sex, sodomy, and intimate kissing and touching. Laws in other states, Minnesota, for example, also prohibit sexual contact with former patients under certain circumstances, particularly when the professional relationship was terminated primarily for the purpose of beginning a sexual relationship (see Chapter 9). Additionally, some of the criminal statutes prohibit sexual intimacy if the patient remains emotionally "dependent" on the therapist, even after termination. This, of course, is difficult to prove but it benefits the patient because it puts the burden on the therapist to show that the patient was not still dependent. The important factor is that the criminal laws are intended to cover virtually all practicing therapists, are intended to prohibit a wide range of sexual behavior, and cover a variety of circumstances.

Sandy had been seeing a social worker, Mr. R., for approximately 6 months when he began to initiate inappropriate sexual conduct. Several times when her session was over he would stand so that she had to squeeze by him in order to leave. On another occasion, during a session when she was very upset about something that had happened during the week, he approached her and kissed her in an erotic way, later claiming that it was an aspect of his method of therapy.

In those states that have not made sexual exploitation a criminal offense, cases of sexual misconduct are still occasionally prosecuted as criminal acts if the conduct was extreme. For example, if a patient was approached by the therapist in a sexual way and refused or otherwise objected to the advances, and he persisted by forcing himself on her, she might be able to charge him with the criminal offense of rape. Similarly, if sexual contact was made without her knowledge (e.g., during hypnosis) or because under the circumstances she was unable to consent (e.g., as a minor or incompetent person), a rape charge would be appropriate. For example, in a California case in the early 1960s a psychiatrist was convicted under a statutory rape law for having sexual contact with an underaged (16-year-old) girl. This is the exception, however, as few cases are prosecuted criminally except in those eleven states in which a specific law is in effect. In fact, there is a great reluctance among both patients and law enforcement agencies to pursue criminal charges against therapists who engage in sexual misconduct.

Most of the specific statutes that make therapist-patient sexual contact a criminal offense classify the conduct as a felony, which is the most serious type of criminal act. Despite this, the penalties for sexual misconduct vary. In Colorado, for example, the criminal statute looks at the type of sexual act performed and imposes a lesser penalty for "sexual contact" than for "sexual penetration." Other statutes provide lesser penalties for a first violation and stiffer penalties for subsequent violations. In California, for example, a first offense is a "misdemeanor," which is a lesser criminal offense than a felony. In Florida, all offenses are felonies but the "degree" (and thus the penalty) increases when there is a subsequent conviction.

The penalties imposed under the various laws depend upon the statute and the seriousness of the offense, but they range from "up to 5 years" in prison to "up to 15 years" in prison and fines from "up to $5,000" to "up to $30,000." In all cases the sentencing judge has the discretion to determine the penalty within the guidelines provided by the statute. He or she often exercises substantial discretion to impose a just penalty.

IS CONSENT A DEFENSE?

The question of whether it should even be considered that a patient might have somehow "consented" to sexual contact with the mental health professional has been hotly debated. Because of the nature of the relationship, most victims do, in fact, "consent" and may even encourage sexual intimacy. Nevertheless, as discussed in Chapter 2, this is not "true" consent because patients are generally unfamiliar with transference phenomena and generally do not recognize that what they experience as "love" is actually a transference reaction. Therefore, whatever "consent" there is results from unrealistic feelings of intimacy and affection which are part of the process of psychotherapy and are knowingly and intentionally elicited by the therapist. Consequently, most courts, civil and criminal, recognize that whether or not a patient may have voluntarily participated in her own exploitation does not affect the ethical obligation of the therapist not to take advantage of her.

When Dr. S. was charged with improper sexual contact with a patient, he defended himself on the basis that she had initiated the

relationship and that he resisted her sexual advances. He sought to
testify that it was only when she had threatened to attempt suicide
if he rejected her that he ultimately consented to a sexual relationship because he thought it was necessary to keep his patient alive.

Most criminal statutes do not, in fact, even allow the defendant (therapist) to assert "consent" as a defense to the criminal prosecution. On the
civil side, many courts will consider whether the patient "consented" to
whatever conduct occurred but will also consider the circumstances of
the consent, particularly the transference issues.

Although eliminating "consent" as a defense to sexual exploitation
would seem to be a great benefit to victims, its effect has been mixed.
As more states consider criminal legislation, a number are troubled by
the inference that any person who consults a mental health professional
must, for legal purposes, be treated as a child, mentally and legally
incapable of saying "no." The answer seems to be that even a competent
and capable adult is vulnerable to undue influence under certain circumstances, and this is presumed to be one of them.

Those states which have criminal laws that make sexual exploitation
illegal have them because they consider it to be a serious and complex
problem which they believe can best be addressed in this way. Many
women are particularly vulnerable because of past histories of sexual
abuse and other difficult clinical problems that leave them easily exploited. Some actually appear seductive. An ethical therapist will recognize and treat this behavior for what it is and see it as a resource to be
used to perform the services for which he was engaged. Those who use
this opportunity to exploit patients cause further damage in the very area
in which they are most needy and vulnerable. They do so knowingly and
intentionally. Many states believe that criminal laws are an appropriate
sanction for such misconduct.

There are several benefits to the victim in having a criminal law that
punishes sexual misconduct. First, it is anticipated that at least some of
the therapists who are prone to exploiting their patients will be deterred
by criminal penalties. Second, criminal prosecution does not depend
upon an unsuspecting patient to file a lawsuit. Once such a patient dis-
cusses the sexual misconduct with anyone, including a new therapist, it
may be reported to the criminal authorities. She may not even know
about it. Thus the threat of heavy fines, imprisonment, and a criminal
"record" is greater than the threat of a "mere" civil suit.

For the victim, criminal penalties do not yield any direct benefit in that she gets no financial award. But for some victims, it is more important to their well-being to see the abuser punished, even imprisoned. Victims of exploitation often are left with unresolved feelings of shame and guilt about their participation in the sexual relationship. Making such conduct by a therapist criminal places the "blame" where it belongs and helps resolve some of those feelings of shame and guilt. At the same time, if a therapist is found guilty in the criminal case, it will make it almost certain that the patient will win the later civil suit because guilt has already been established.

It is important to realize that it is almost certain that an accuser will be called upon to testify against the therapist in a criminal case. Because the stakes are so high, most therapists do not admit to sexual misconduct, and the accuser, as the "star" witness, will be expected to prove that it happened. She can expect that the therapist's lawyer will attempt to discredit her, using anything that the therapist can tell him to cast doubt on her credibility. Patients of psychotherapy are sitting ducks for having their credibility attacked, and they have to expect that whatever the therapist knows might be used as ammunition. In the end the personal toll that a criminal trial takes can be enormous. Sometimes this actually aids a victim's recovery process, but too often it is an unpleasant experience she never forgets.

Society may also benefit from criminal laws against sexual exploitation, at least to the extent that it prevents abusive therapists from harming other patients. Once a criminal prosecution occurs, it is likely that a proceeding before the state licensing board, attempting to revoke the therapist's license, will follow. Local publicity is likely. The intent is that the general public, particularly those who engage mental health professionals, better understand the problem and avoid becoming the next victim.

Not surprisingly, there are also drawbacks in making sexual exploitation a criminal offense. Among the most significant is the possibility that reporting will actually be deterred because the stakes are so high for the offender. Many therapists are more willing to report offending colleagues when they know that the purpose is to "rehabilitate" rather than severely punish them. If the penalty is imprisonment, some will be more reluctant to report an offense. Some victims may also be deterred from reporting by the requirements of the criminal law. Even though the victim does not make the decision to prosecute, she has to participate in a criminal prosecution and her willingness to do so greatly affects the success of the case.

The victim's willingness to participate in a criminal prosecution is something that she must consider seriously. Is she prepared to have her privacy invaded? Is she strong enough to publicize her victimization? In too many cases, victims are too fragile to undergo a criminal prosecution and it actually causes more harm than good, including impeding recovery. Instead of getting relief from those feelings of guilt and shame, if she is not ready to deal with the powerful emotions that arise, she may feel worse.

Yet another pitfall of the criminal process is that if the victim is contemplating bringing a civil lawsuit (which, unlike the criminal case, *does* benefit her) she may be deterred after going through the truly grueling process of a criminal prosecution. In the criminal case, she doubtless will have to testify and be cross-examined about her sexual conduct with the therapist. If this process is really traumatic, as it can be, she may not be willing to subject herself to the legal system yet again, even to obtain compensation for the harm done to her.

> The therapist who sexually abused Jennifer was reported to the authorities by a friend of hers and was prosecuted in a criminal court. Jennifer was subpoenaed to testify. When the therapist's lawyer was entitled to cross-examine Jennifer, he grilled her over and over again about how she dressed and what she said and forced her to describe, in painful detail, exactly what kind of advances and sexual conduct occurred. The therapist was ultimately convicted, and Jennifer was advised that winning the civil lawsuit to "pay" her for what was done would be easy. After having been traumatized by the criminal trial, Jennifer refused to submit to the legal process again, even though it would be an easier case, and even though it might help her pay for subsequent therapy.

Probably the most troubling aspect of the criminal law is its inability to distinguish between those therapists who habitually and intentionally exploit and abuse their patients as long as they can get away with it, and those who unwittingly allow it to happen once and are better rehabilitated than punished.

> Dr. K. had been a therapist for 33 years. Within that period, he had engaged in sexual relationships with more than twenty women. According to him, he was never involved with more than one at a time and he only became involved when he believed that it would

benefit the patient. In fact, the vast majority were devastated by the experience and several became suicidal. He continued to practice this type of "therapy," however, until he was finally reported and prosecuted by his state, which made sexual misconduct of psychotherapists a criminal offense.

Dr. B. had practiced psychotherapy for 26 years and always believed that sexual contact with a patient was strictly forbidden. However, at the age of 52 and in the midst of a divorce, he found himself increasingly attracted to a patient who initiated a social relationship with him. She suggested that her "therapy" could be finished and that such a relationship would be of great benefit to both of them. Dr. B. rationalized that since he would be seeing her, he could determine whether she needed more therapy and refer her to a colleague if needed. Soon after they began a sexual relationship, Dr. B. recognized that the patient did, indeed, need further treatment. He also realized that her attraction to him had to be sorted out and that his sexual relationship with her prevented her from getting the necessary treatment.

To a large extent, the criminal statutes are not able to make meaningful distinctions between those who need to be rehabilitated, those who need to be deterred, and those who need to be punished. But for an individual victim it probably does not make a lot of difference, and the criminal law may go a long way toward improving awareness and understanding about sexual exploitation. Those therapists who are capable of rehabilitation should be required to have it; those who are not should be prevented from practicing. The administrative and criminal alternatives outlined in this chapter indicate that this problem is increasingly being taken seriously and that its consequences are recognized as real. No one remedy has proved to be a perfect solution, but along with the civil options discussed in the following chapter, the recourse available to victims reflects an awareness of the seriousness of the problem.

Chapter 6

Bringing Your Therapist to Court: The Costs and Benefits of Private Lawsuits

In many cases exploited women who seek to pursue their abusers are content to have the licensure board or criminal courts, discussed in the previous chapter, process and act upon their complaints. The consequences to the professional range from private censure and formal disciplinary procedures to loss of license or membership in professional organizations to ultimate imprisonment in some states. Although the vast majority of abusive therapists are never subjected to any formal sanction, the costs to those who are can be enormous. It is not unusual for such a practitioner to be ostracized from the professional community and even to lose his ability to practice and earn a living. Yet there is another, potentially more devastating consequence: the risk of a civil lawsuit. Not only can this result in substantial awards of money damages to a successful victim, but the emotional costs of defending a civil lawsuit can be even greater than those connected with an administrative proceeding. This is now a public forum, unprotected by privileged procedures or confidentiality. This chapter will highlight the civil remedies that may be available to a victim as well as the defenses and obstacles that she may be required to endure.

WHY A LAWSUIT?

Victims of sexual exploitation bring civil lawsuits for monetary recovery for a number of reasons. Sometimes they feel that the administrative sanction, if any, was inadequate punishment for the suffering they experienced. Sometimes they believe that criminal action should have been taken. Sometimes they simply feel that justice is not done if the abuser has suffered no monetary loss. Perhaps they will seek money damages in order to have the resources to secure professional help to deal with the consequences of the exploitation, or to continue whatever services the therapist had been engaged to perform. Some people find that a civil action can be therapeutic, challenging the victim's ability to face her abuser and fight back. In that case, initiating a court action and meeting the abuser face-to-face, often for the first time since the betrayal, are symbolic of the victim's progress toward recovery. Like no other available remedy, the civil lawsuit puts the victim back in control and assures her of the opportunity to be heard.

After Terri was abused and then abandoned by her psychotherapist, she became very depressed and thought she could never bear to see him again. Several weeks after she started new therapy, however, her depression turned to anger as she started to come to grips with the abuse. As the therapy progressed, Terri felt more and more that she was ready to take control of what happened to her and force the psychotherapist to confront her and everyone else and admit what he did.

LEGAL THEORIES AND PROCEDURES

Bringing a civil lawsuit against a therapist who exploits a patient's trust is similar to filing suit against any professional who has caused a personal injury. It begins with a "complaint." This amounts to a statement of what happened between the patient and the offender, along with a brief description of why the law makes him legally accountable for those actions in court. The "legal theory" or basis on which these cases are typically brought depends upon the jurisdiction. Currently four states have passed statutes that provide a legal basis for bringing a civil lawsuit for sexual exploitation: California, Illinois, Minnesota, and Wisconsin. In those states where there is no specific statute, the legal theory generally used today is "malpractice." This means that there was a profes-

There are very few exceptions to the statutes of limitations. One is a legal doctrine known as the "discovery rule." This allows the time the victim has to pursue her claim to be extended if she can prove that she did not, and could not, "discover" the injury within the period prescribed to bring the lawsuit. In those cases most courts are willing to extend the period, giving the victim a reasonable amount of time after she has (or "should have") discovered her injury, to bring suit.

David was treated in June 1984 for a broken ankle. During the evaluation he was accidentally subjected to a very large dose of radiation. The statute of limitations for personal injury was 2 years in his state. However, it was not until February 1992 that any evidence of cancer appeared which could be attributed to the overdose of radiation. The statute of limitations will probably begin in February 1994 and will "run" in February 1996.

Because of the nature of sexual exploitation by therapists and the consequences of transference phenomena, it is entirely possible that a victim may not realize that she has been victimized or recognize the extent of the harm within the prescribed period. It is often not until many years later, perhaps after reentering therapy with another therapist, that she comes to understand that she was a victim of exploitation. Maybe she believed that because she consented or, at very least, did not object to the therapist's sexual advances, she has no claim against the abusive therapist. This, of course, is not the case, but she may not recognize it until after the period has elapsed. A number of courts have been forced to deal with the question of whether the discovery rule should apply under these circumstances.

In the federal lawsuit discussed previously, the victim filed suit nearly 3 years after the abuse began in a state that had a 2-year statute of limitations. The court applied the discovery rule (which is used primarily in medical malpractice actions) and allowed the claim on the basis that the victim did not "discover" the wrong done to her until she consulted a psychiatrist some years later and learned that the exploitation caused her further emotional difficulties.

More recently, in a 1991 case also in Massachusetts, the Supreme Judicial Court held that the statute of limitations would not start to run until a victim knew that she might have been injured by her psychotherapist's misconduct. Recognizing that the causes of psychological injury can be subtle and the behavior is often justified to the patient as proper or acceptable, the court held that the time begins to run when the "reasonable person who ha[d] been subjected to the conduct" would have recognized that she may have been injured by improper conduct.

Defense 2: Informed Consent

The most obvious potential defense to claims of sexual exploitation is that the patient, a legally competent adult, consented to the sexual activity. The theory of informed consent is that both doctor and patient communicate, understand, and respect each other's duties and obligations, particularly those concerning the potential benefits and risks of treatment. Most importantly, it is the patient and not the doctor who ultimately decides what is in her own best interest. In some cases, however, particularly those in which there is a substantial imbalance of power, the doctor has a special obligation if he believes that she may be highly susceptible to influence and not really capable of giving fully informed consent. Part of the obligation is to exercise particular care. In psychotherapy, the patient consents to an initial, provisional treatment plan, but she is not likely to understand her evolving experience of the treatment, particularly the transference phenomenon. As a result, therapists must recognize that, as to treatment issues involving transference, even an intelligent, capable person can be unduly influenced. Consequently, there is no true informed consent. Special care is necessary so as not to manipulate, abuse, or exploit the transference relationship.

> Kerry was referred to Dr. A. by her family doctor for treatment of depression. After several weeks of therapy, she began to feel better about herself and started to develop strong feelings of attraction toward Dr. A. In fact, it was she who pursued him and suggested that she wanted to have a sexual relationship with him. Her expression of affection seemed sincere and Dr. A. had developed feelings of his own for Kerry.

At this point it is up to the doctor to recognize the transference, be willing to work through it with the patient, but at the same time be clear and unequivocal that he will not now, nor at any future time, have any sort of sexual contact with the patient.

At the onset of the professional relationship, prior to any transference involvement, patients "bargain for" therapeutic treatment, not a sexual relationship. If, as therapists acknowledge, the transference renders true voluntary consent impossible because of the issues that develop, then informed consent about acting on transference feelings (such as agreeing to, or even initiating sexual contact with the therapist) is virtually meaningless.

Defense 3: Contributory Negligence

A similar but not identical legal concept that the courts have addressed is a principle known as "contributory negligence." A victim is contributorily negligent if she somehow voluntarily contributes to her own injury, whether or not her participation is intentional.

Michael was walking against a traffic light when he was hit by a car which was speeding. Because of excessive speed, the driver was unable to stop. The driver is likely to be found "negligent" for driving too fast, but Michael may be found "contributorily negligent" for walking against the traffic light. Depending on the state and how much Michael "contributed" to his injury, his award may be either reduced or denied.

Is a patient contributorily negligent in being sexually exploited if she "consents" to or even initiates sexual contact with her therapist? The mental health professions are unequivocal in saying "no." They insist that the power structure and transference dynamics are so important that there can be no voluntary consent, under virtually any circumstances. With respect to the law, most civil courts will admit and consider evidence of the surrounding circumstances for possible contributory negligence. This could include, for example, her knowledge that the therapist was married and therefore the sexual contact was illicit. Furthermore, in those states where criminal statutes exist, consent is irrelevant and not a defense.

In practice, courts today usually recognize the tranference phenomenon as a valid principle and ultimately do not accept either informed consent or contributory negligence as a defense. Nevertheless, it seems illogical that if a patient agrees to a sexual relationship (and appears in court to be legally competent) that nonetheless she was, in fact, psychologically incapable of giving informed consent. The practical consequence in the civil actions is that her psychological and sexual history is put on display in an attempt to discredit her claim. Courts are notoriously slow in demonstrating the understanding and sensitivity that would be required to overcome this conceptual hurdle: that is, recognizing that a woman who is in all other respects capable and competent to make informed decisions can nevertheless be so unduly influenced that she loses her ability to make this voluntary, informed decision in a rational manner. This would shield her from having to put her psychological and sexual history on display, instead allowing the transference phenomenon to be set forth to explain her participation.

DAMAGES (COMPENSATION FOR THE VICTIM)

The final legal obstacle that a victim must overcome is proving that she was injured or damaged as a result of the sexual relationship with her therapist. The purpose of civil lawsuits is only to compensate victims for harm actually suffered. Consequently, an important part of her "case" is her ability to prove that she was injured or "damaged" by the acts of the accused therapist. In cases of sexual exploitation, the resulting harm is often difficult to demonstrate or explain to a jury. The best way of doing so is to bring in another therapist who has since evaluated the victim and can explain the harm that was done.

In addition to the legal theories discussed earlier, courts often recognize a legal claim known as "negligent (or intentional) infliction of emotional distress." This means that in committing the wrong, the accused negligently or intentionally caused emotional suffering. This "emotional distress" aspect of the claim is largely what results in monetary awards, since there is often no physical injury. The dollar value of emotional distress is highly subjective and may depend upon the victim's ability to communicate the real impact of the harm suffered effectively.

What are the elements of emotional distress that a jury can consider? These may include overwhelming feelings of guilt, abandonment, anger, sexual dysfunction, inability to trust, and, not infrequently, risk of suicide.

A final item of the monetary award that is allowed by some courts is known as "punitive" damages. Particularly in those cases in which the other damages are inadequate to punish a defendant, a court might impose punitive damages for egregious, willful, wanton, reckless, or outrageous behavior.

Elizabeth was sexually exploited by her psychotherapist and successfully sued him for her injuries. The jury found that she suffered from emotional distress as a result of his conduct. Her "injury" included sexual dysfunction and undue feelings of anger and abandonment. The jury awarded $10,000 for treatment with a subsequent therapist, $30,000 for "compensation" for her emotional distress, and $50,000 in "punitive" damages to punish the abusive conduct.

Juries will award damages to a sympathetic victim who can prove that she suffered as a result of being exploited. The dollar value of these cases is highly unpredictable, depending on the makeup of the jury and the presentation of the case. Low damage awards can be increased with punitive damages; on the other hand, the court may also be able to reduce an award which it believes to be excessive. In the case that occurred in New York discussed previously, the court reduced a $100,000 award to $25,000 on the basis that the victim's psychological condition as it existed prior to the sexual violation was severe, and its award should reflect only the aggravation of that condition. Nevertheless, many courts' attitudes toward sexual exploitation have changed considerably since that decision and even multimillion-dollar awards have been seen today.

LIABILITY OF EMPLOYERS

A final issue that has confronted a number of courts is the question of whether the employer of an abusive therapist should be legally responsible to a victim of sexual exploitation. If, for example, a patient goes to a mental health agency and is exploited by the therapist assigned to her, is the agency liable? Not surprisingly, the courts are not consistent in the way that they treat this issue. On the one hand, employers are generally liable for acts of their employees which occur within the scope of the employment. On the other hand, employers are generally not liable for intentional or illicit acts which do not necessarily occur as a consequence of the employment. Of course, the employer would argue that it neither authorized nor even knew about the exploitation.

In the federal matter discussed previously, the federal appeals court upheld an award of $150,000 on the basis that the sexual relationship between therapist and patient could not be understood apart from the therapeutic relationship: Although the sexual aspect was clearly not within the "scope" of the therapist's duties, it nevertheless "arose out of" the practice of an employee. The employer was therefore considered liable for the acts of its employee.

An alternative theory has been used in arguments against employers in those cases in which the court has found that the sexual relationship was outside the scope of employment and therefore not the responsibility of the employer. In a case in Colorado, a court held that although an employer should not be held liable for an illegal or forbidden act of its employee, it could be liable for negligent hiring or supervision of that employee. That case involved a parish priest who had previously been known by the diocese to have sexually exploited other parishioners and had done nothing about it.

> Dr. K. was employed by Tri-State Mental Health Services. A jury found that he had sexually exploited a patient and awarded her $25,000 in damages. Tri-State was also named as a defendant on the basis that it employed Dr. K. and that it should have better supervised his activities. Tri-State defended itself on the basis that (1) sexual contact with patients was illegal in its state and (2) that it occurred away from the employer's premises. Depending on the state and on whether or not Tri-State had any reason to know that Dr. K. was abusing his patients, the employer may or may not be liable.

Like the administrative and regulatory mechanisms discussed in the previous chapter, so far the civil law seems to have done relatively little to curb the problem of sexual exploitation among therapists. Clearly a large part of the problem, which also serves to discourage victims from coming forward, is the erratic enforcement. Most abusive therapists know that the probability of getting caught and being held accountable is reliably low. Many also expect to be shielded by the unspoken "conspiracy of silence" between professionals whereby each is very reluctant to speak out against another. Nevertheless, the consequences to the few can be severe and, even if a therapist is ultimately absolved of the charges, the judicial and administrative proceedings are demanding and certain to take an enormous toll.

Chapter 7

Legal Recourse for Sexual Exploitation by Other Professionals: The Emerging Law

CASE STUDY: LORI

I was referred to attorney Jeff K. by a girlfriend who was divorced three-and-one-half years earlier. Jeff had gotten her a fabulous settlement and I was scared to death about facing my husband, Dave, in court. When I didn't jump at his first offer of half the house and nothing else, Dave hinted that he might try to take my children away. When I heard about how Jeff always got what he wanted for his clients, I knew that I desperately needed him to take my case.

When I first met Jeff I was immediately struck by his smooth and gentle manner. He gave me the impression that he absolutely knew what he was doing and that he cared about getting good results for his clients. I was delighted when he agreed to take my case. He asked for $2,500 up front, which my girlfriend told me was the usual "retainer." I didn't know exactly what that meant but I assumed it at least meant that he was stuck with me. I certainly felt a lot better knowing that Jeff was handling the divorce.

Thinking back, one thing that surprised me was that a couple of times Dave's lawyer inquired about a reconciliation and both times Jeff immediately dismissed the possibility, without asking me what I thought or even giving it serious consideration. I rationalized it at the time as trial strategy, but I kept wondering whether he would ever ask me about it. In fact, Jeff often made decisions about the case for me, and I figured that it was how he managed to get such great results. I also sort of admired a man who would take charge and felt that I was in good hands.

Right from the beginning there were so many things that I liked about Jeff. He was good-looking, but not in a flashy way. His personality was almost a Jekyll and Hyde in that he was kind and patient with me and such a tough fighter when he dealt with Dave's lawyer. I think that that's probably what I liked the most about him: I knew he could get what he wanted. Also, right from the beginning Jeff gave me the sense that somehow my case was special, that he really cared about my getting those kids, and that he really cared about me.

The third time I met with Jeff he asked me to go out for a drink afterward. He didn't try to pressure me. He just said that it would be good for both of us to unwind and that he enjoyed my company and would like to spend a little more time to get to know me. He was a perfect gentleman that evening and whatever reluctance I felt when he first asked soon disappeared. I had a great time and I got a little better glimpse of that Jekyll and Hyde personality, but in a way that made me more comfortable. He seemed to say that there was him and there was his work, and that as a litigator, he needed to maintain a tough facade. But he assured me that the real Jeff was the kind and gentle man I knew and I ate it all up.

It was only a matter of weeks before Jeff and I were seeing each other regularly and we quickly became involved sexually. Having Jeff in my corner made me feel secure and having him pay attention to me and love me made it much easier to get through the divorce. But to tell the truth, a part of me was afraid to think too much about what was going on. Sometimes he would make references to our future together, but I really couldn't see beyond getting divorced from Dave. In any event I didn't want to rock the boat because I was desperately afraid of losing the kids.

After about 8 torturous months Jeff and my husband's lawyer started serious negotiations. Now I needed Jeff more than ever because all kinds of confusing proposals were being kicked around and I had no idea what some of them meant or even what was best for me. Did I want alimony or a larger share of the house? If I agreed to joint custody, what would happen if Dave decided to move out of town? I was in no condition to think through the consequences of these things and I needed to rely on Jeff to do what was right.

Right before the holidays of that year we were close to settlement and Dave even seemed a little more generous about my share of the house. But he was dead set against alimony and I didn't think I could make it with just the income from my part-time job. The house was going to be sold, but who knew when or how much it would bring. I looked to Jeff for those answers and in his typical self-confident way, he just kept telling me not to worry. He said I should be grateful that Dave wasn't fighting for the children and besides, alimony would probably end if I remarried or lived with another man. Well, I had no thought of remarrying but I did know that the bills had to be paid every month. When we got to the final negotiation, Dave's lawyer was adamant about the great settlement he was offering and Jeff was really pressuring me to take it. I was confused and I was scared, and when Dave mumbled something (I don't even know what) about the kids, I just grabbed the offer, frightened as I was.

Right from the start I regretted taking that deal. I was relieved that there was no fight over the children, but scared that I didn't have adequate income to support them. I also found out later that once alimony was waived in the original settlement, it was virtually impossible to get it later. Things ended up in a mess. The house didn't sell for over a year and I had to get a full-time job just to make ends meet. Dave paid some child support, but it wasn't reliable and it barely covered the extra day care since I had to work so many more hours. Of course, I don't know what else might have been possible, but I've always wondered what might have happened if I had held out for alimony.

What happened to Jeff? Our relationship lasted for about 3 months after the divorce when he told me that he really wanted to marry me. For me, it was much too soon to think about a commitment to another man, particularly since my children needed me more than ever and the demands of my new job were already affecting my ability to care for them. When I told Jeff that I wasn't ready and couldn't think about marriage now, he said something that floored me: "How do you think you're going to make it with no husband and no alimony?" he demanded to know. It wasn't until that moment that I realized what I think I may have understood all along: Jeff had his own agenda, and if I married him, I would have been better off forgoing alimony and taking a larger share of the property since alimony would end when I remarried anyway.

The fact was that marrying Jeff at that time wasn't in the cards for me. As I think back on it, I dated him mostly because I was afraid to say "no." Of course, there was a part of me that liked Jeff and was turned on by his kind manner, his powerful position, and his obvious interest in me. At the time, I needed his strength, but after the divorce, I was more interested in taking care of my children and developing my own supports. Jeff helped me a lot but he never told me that the settlement that he recommended only worked if I went along with his plans for me to marry him. I didn't, and my children and I paid the price for many years to come.

For years the mental health professions have been plagued with the knowledge that many practitioners within their ranks have taken advantage of unsuspecting patients by engaging them in sexual relationships. For a long time, little was said and less was done. However, in recent years the professions themselves, recognizing the magnitude of the problem and the severity of the consequences to victims, have taken a visible role in denouncing and punishing such conduct. As sexual exploitation became better understood in that field, many of the other professions were also forced to examine the conduct of their own members. Not surprisingly, remarkably similar occurrences were found, as was a new trail of victims. Some other professions have been slower to respond, however, but in recent years they, too, have been forced to come to terms with this widespread problem.

ATTORNEYS

The legal profession has recently received substantial publicity concerning sexual exploitation among lawyers, particularly divorce lawyers. In 1992 the state of California declared a "ban" on lawyer/client sexual relations while the lawyer is representing the client, *if* the relationship affects the quality of the legal services. The prohibition provided little guidance about how the representation might be affected, although ethics boards had addressed that issue on numerous occasions. Shortly after California adopted its position, Oregon followed suit, also prohibiting lawyer/client sexual relations. At the same time Illinois was carefully reviewing a similar regulation, although it has yet to take action as this book goes to press. No actual cases have yet tested the application of the new California or Oregon rules, although numerous cases covering the same matter have been the subject of disciplinary proceedings throughout the country. California has a civil remedy for sexual exploitation in addition to its already existing administrative (disciplinary) ac-

tion, including the removal or suspension of a member's license to practice law.

Unlike psychotherapists, who identify a specific therapeutic process
(transference) as responsible for their ability to exert undue influence on
their patients, lawyers are less exact about what it is about the lawyer-
client relationship that can result in similar undue influence. What has
been said is that there is a power imbalance (i.e., the lawyer knows more
about how to handle the legal matter than the client) which requires
the client to place his trust and confidence in his lawyer. As the more
knowledgeable person, the lawyer therefore becomes more influential.
This is traditionally known as a "fiduciary" relationship in which one
individual seeks the services of another simply because an "expert" in
the field is needed to assist the layperson in making independent, informed judgments about what is in her best interest. As a result, she
hires an expert, the lawyer, whom she, as the client, must then trust.
She may reveal to him highly confidential information, even sometimes
including a confession of criminal conduct, with confidence and faith
that the lawyer will use this information only to assist her and always
act in her best interest.

Is this a transference or transferencelike relationship? The answer appears to be that it has many of the same features of the special relationship which is technically reserved for mental health professionals. Although it is less obvious, the transferencelike relationship may occur in
a very compelling way. Transference feelings can result when one person (the client or patient) views another person as being in a more powerful role, akin to that of a parent, and experiences (even acts out) feelings of unquestioning trust, dependency, and need. In theory, what seem
to make the lawyer/client relationship less compelling are that the dependency and need are not necessarily of an emotional nature and that
emotional involvement with the client is not necessary in order for the
attorney to perform his services. Often, but not always, the issues are of
a practical nature (real estate transactions, preparing a will). As a result,
the attorney's client is more likely to be able to make a judgment about
whether she welcomes emotional involvement with her lawyer. But not
necessarily.

Lawyers often deal with emotionally troubling circumstances such as
divorces and personal injury, as well as with emotionally distraught clients. They also deal with clients who are ignorant about their option to
find another (nonabusive) lawyer. Lawyers deal with clients who are
scared or intimidated about their circumstances (whatever their entangle-

ment with the law might be). Lawyers also deal with clients who have dependent personalities and/or who are afraid to say "no" if approached with an inappropriate or unwelcome request (for example, for sexual intimacy) by their attorney. While it is unclear how much transference may be involved in a particular case, what is certain is that at least the fiduciary obligation owed to these clients includes the duty not to require, coerce, or cajole them into a sexual relationship.

The question of whether lawyers, like psychotherapists, should have a legal as well as a moral obligation to recognize undue dependency and not take advantage of it is a more difficult one. Unlike psychotherapists, lawyers are not trained to recognize and deal with transference and countertransference phenomena. Of course, lawyers *could* be trained to understand enough to recognize transferencelike reactions: how they occur and how to deal with them. Lawyers *could* certainly be trained to understand that when a dependent or needy client confronts a kind and attentive professional who undertakes to pursue her cause zealously certain transferencelike feelings can arise. They *could* also be trained to understand that clients who are in an emotionally vulnerable state (as when going through a divorce) are more prone to transference reactions. They *can* also come to understand that certain rules of professional conduct result from this occurrence. The real problem is that, in practice, transference is more complicated to understand and address by one untrained in mental health. The prelude to sexual involvement is often complicated. It is not always possible for an untrained professional to recognize the inappropriate precursors to exploitative conduct. And so the result is that lawyers find themselves on the brink of prohibited conduct, searching for excuses or rationalizing their behavior because they never understood why they were at risk for becoming the perpetrators of sexual exploitation.

The alternative to requiring lawyers to understand and deal with transference phenomena is simply to require them to understand what it means to abuse a fiduciary relationship. All professionals can be expected to recognize that when their clients have to place their blind faith and trust in them, they must not abuse that trust. Then it is only a small leap to prohibit the professional from engaging in any kind of relationship with a client that might influence or impair the client's free will. In fact, all professions have adopted a code of ethics that operates to do just that. Psychotherapists have specifically identified sexual relations as, per se, such an activity. Other professions are beginning to reach the same conclusion. Numerous cases have been brought under legal standards of ethics when lawyers have influenced or coerced a client, engaging them in sexual relations.

> Atty. G. was a divorce lawyer. Sharon was his client. Atty. G. was kind and attentive to Sharon's case and she was emotionally vulnerable. At one point Atty. G. told Sharon that he was sexually attracted to her. She submitted to his advances, uncertain whether she, too, was attracted to him (e.g., was she attracted to *him,* or to his position and his interest and attentiveness to her?) She was certain that she didn't want to lose him as her lawyer and wasn't sure what would happen if she declined his sexual advances.

In a Wisconsin case an attorney was accused of suddenly asking a client to remove her clothes while they were meeting in his office. When she refused, he turned off the lights and began to fondle her. Without citing a specific rule, the Wisconsin Supreme Court upheld a 90-day license suspension on the basis that there was an ethical obligation binding attorneys that prohibited unsolicited sexual contact.

Another common situation occurred in an Iowa case. An attorney was accused of kissing and fondling an inmate whom he was assigned to represent. An Iowa court said that the lawyer had an ethical obligation to behave in a professional manner. The court determined that his conduct was not "temperate and dignified" as required by the code of ethics, and he received a reprimand.

More recently, two highly publicized cases occurred in New England, one in New Hampshire and one in Rhode Island. In the New Hampshire case a 34-year-old married woman sued her divorce lawyer for engaging her in a "consensual" sexual relationship with him while he was representing her in the divorce action. The woman had been under the care of a psychiatrist for treatment of a mental condition. On three occasions beginning within a week of meeting this client the lawyer initiated sexual contact with her, professing great attraction and claiming that he, too, was experiencing a deteriorating marriage. When in due course the lawyer terminated the sexual relationship, the client was left with only a hope that somehow their relationship might be salvaged.

With a significantly deteriorated emotional state and the urging of a compassionate psychiatrist, the woman was eventually able to find a new lawyer and she initiated both a complaint before the New Hampshire Bar Association and a private lawsuit. The disciplinary proceeding before the bar association was heard first; there it was determined that a sexual relationship did, in fact, occur (contrary to the denial of the lawyer). As for whether or not she consented: that did not matter, said the court. The lawyer knew that she was in an "emotionally fragile" state and was under treatment for a mental disability, and it violated his "fiduciary" (professional) obligation to her when he preyed on her known vulnerability and engaged her in a sexual relationship. In the lawsuit that followed, a jury awarded her $125,000 for the emotional pain and suffering that resulted from the lawyer's unethical conduct.

A short time later the case in Rhode Island was heard. In that case another woman also sued her divorce lawyer for engaging her in a sexual relationship with him. She, too, claimed to be in an emotionally compromised situation as she dealt with a difficult divorce. Furthermore, in that case the lawyer's law partners were also sued on the grounds that they knew of the improper sexual relationship and reportedly looked the other way.

Numerous other cases have been brought around the country for sexual misconduct and exploitation at the hands of lawyers. In the past penalties generally included private or public censure, reprimand, suspension of license, and outright disbarment (loss of license to practice law). Recently, however, they have also included the possibility of a private lawsuit brought by a client who claims to have been injured as a result of the improper conduct.

While disciplinary proceedings against lawyers for unethical sexual misconduct have been numerous, civil suits are still relatively rare. The legal basis for such suits against psychotherapists is usually "malpractice," since the therapist is thought to mishandle the transference phenomenon, which is a specific part of the psychological treatment. That legal theory is more difficult to apply to lawyers since managing transference is not a recognized part of legal practice. Instead the basis for a malpractice action is that lawyers are usually said to breach their fiduciary obligations to clients when they engage in sexual misconduct.

The idea that a lawyer who sexually exploits a client might be sued civilly on that basis is quite new. In fact, the first case brought against a lawyer for sexual exploitation as a basis for legal malpractice was tried in California in 1983. In that case the plaintiff brought suit alleging legal malpractice, fraud, battery, and intentional misrepresentation on the basis that she had agreed to engage in sexual relations with the defendant (her attorney) only when he said that he "[couldn't] possibly get anyone pregnant." The plaintiff did, in fact, become pregnant, with substantial resulting physical complications. The court said that the at-

DOCTORS

Yet another clear opportunity for sexual exploitation arises in the context of nonpsychiatric doctor/patient relationships. In these cases sexual contact is initiated by the physician during or after medical treatment. Such relationships often occur in one of several ways. In some cases, sexual conduct is recommended as part of treatment. For example, this might occur among practitioners known as "sex therapists" or other practitioners who purport to treat sexual dysfunction or other sexual disorders. Without commenting on the ethics or effectiveness of sex therapy, it becomes exploitation when a patient presents herself to a practitioner for a specific problem or treatment and is somehow coerced into submitting to sexual conduct which is not therapeutic and is not intended to benefit her.

In other cases the sexual contact is perpetrated as part of medical treatment, sometimes during an obstetric or gynecological evaluation. For example, a relatively common complaint is that a gynecologist might touch a patient during an examination, manipulating her genitals in a sexual way. In a number of cases, gynecologists have been accused of other types of sexual contact, both oral and genital, including sexual intercourse.

It is important to note that in cases of gynecological malpractice, as in psychiatric malpractice, most courts have held that the sexual misconduct "arises out of" the medical practice, such that it is usually considered "malpractice" and not a separate act of some sort of sexual abuse. Yet in most other (nonpsychiatric) medical contexts sexual misconduct is more likely to be considered abuse or exploitation than malpractice. This is important because a physician's medical liability insurance may cover the claim if the sexual misconduct is labeled "malpractice," but generally will not cover situations that are labeled "exploitation" or "abuse."

The remaining cases, not involving psychotherapy or gynecological services, are more difficult to prove as being inherently exploitative. As discussed in Chapter 3, the imbalance of power and the necessary trust that a patient places in her physician creates a particular professional or "fiduciary" responsibility of the physician. This duty requires that he not use the faith and trust placed in him to extract favors, sexual or otherwise, from a patient who is entitled to believe that he is acting in her best interest or who may be intimidated by his power and thus afraid to say "no."

In a 1992 Massachusetts case, the court addressed the question of whether a dentist's sexual abuse of a woman during dental treatment somehow "arose out of" his professional practice. The court specifically noted that in contrast to the transference phenomenon that occurs in the psychotherapeutic context, "there is nothing inherent in the typical relationship between patient and dentist that makes the patient unusually susceptible to accept the sexual advances of the dentist." The woman argued that his "extremely gentle and caring" manner (particularly for someone who was afraid of dental treatment) made the sexual abuse "intertwined" with the special care that the patient sought from the dentist. The court did not agree and denied her claim that the sexual misconduct "arose out of" the dental treatment.

What is clear from the Massachusetts case is that the patient was arguing that some sort of transferencelike phenomenon had occurred between her and the dentist, brought about by the interaction of his professional stature, his kind and gentle manner, and her vulnerability—her fear of dental treatment. While the court declined to acknowledge any validity to her argument, what was important to the patient was not whether the dentist was guilty of sexual misconduct; the existence of the sexual relationship was established. What the patient wanted to prove was that the conduct "arose out of" the dentist's treatment of her so that his malpractice insurance might ultimately pay the bill.

It is not clear yet whether courts will be inclined to recognize and apply transference theory to cases other than those involving psychotherapy. It is difficult to deny that power imbalance involving an authority figure and a vulnerable patient, along with the need for that patient to trust the authority figure (here, the doctor), contributes greatly to a patient's feeling dependent and submissive. Whether this is labeled specifically as a "transference" occurrence as it is in the mental health field is not the important issue. What is important is the notion that a special relationship is created in which one person (the more powerful party) is in a unique position to exploit his power by extracting sexual favors from the other person (the less powerful party), who trusts his motives and depends upon his acting in her best interest.

Sexual relationships between doctors and patients (other than those in the mental health field) which appear to be both voluntary and consensual have thus far not been considered. Is a consensual sexual relationship with a physician, even during the course of medical treatment, something which the law should regulate? There is no clear answer to this. The medical profession specifically prohibits sexual relationships objected and eventually reported the incident. The teacher sued when the college dismissed him, but the court upheld the dismissal on the basis that the teacher's conduct was immoral and warranted the harsh penalty of dismissal.

In another case an Iowa teacher was terminated for engaging in a sexual relationship with a high school student even though the teacher denied sexual contact and there was no direct evidence that it had occurred. The school board considered the credibility of the teacher and student and also the results of a polygraph (lie detector) test taken by the student. The court upheld the school's dismissal of the teacher even without direct evidence of the student's charges.

In yet another case, an Arizona school dismissed a teacher when a teenage student's parent reported that the teacher had engaged in an improper relationship with the student. The school district dismissed the teacher, not only on the basis that the relationship occurred, but that the teacher had thereafter lied when the charges were being investigated. The teacher defended himself on the basis that the charges pertained to his personal life. The court upheld the dismissal on grounds that the conduct also related to the teacher's role as teacher. The school had a legitimate interest in determining whether he had acted improperly, particularly since, if the conduct was illegal, the school might have been held responsible. Ultimately, however, the dismissal was based upon the teacher's refusal to cooperate with the investigation of the school board.

When sexual exploitation occurs under circumstances that are coercive to the student, the conduct of the teacher might amount to sexual harassment. The cases involving instances of sexual harassment within schools and particular colleges and universities are numerous. "Sexual harassment" usually takes one of two forms. The first is known as "quid pro quo" (literally "something for something"). Here students are approached by teachers or other authority figures (administrators, tutors, etc.) and offered "something" in exchange for sexual favors. The "something" might be a better grade, a better recommendation for graduate school or employment, or some other favor that the authority figure is in a position to grant.

The second form of sexual harassment is known as " 'hostile' or 'poisoned' environment." In these cases the student is subjected to repeated instances of sexual invitations, references, innuendos, or perhaps offensive jokes, pictures, gestures, conduct, or remarks. Unless the conduct is severe, it may not amount to harassment until the student makes it clear that the conduct is offensive and unwelcome and tries, unsuccessfully, to stop it. Sexual harassment is considered to be a form of illegal sex discrimination and victims may be able to sue the offender as well as the institution that employs him.

Unlike consensual relationships between faculty and students, sexual harassment is overtly coercive and offensive and does not require victims to prove that some sort of inherent vulnerability was exploited in order to secure consent. While sexual harassment is now recognized to be a major problem within schools and universities, sexual exploitation is also becoming an increasingly serious concern. Schools are just beginning to address it in a serious way, and recourse available to victims depends upon the particular code of conduct, the state laws, and the circumstances of the case. There are, however, a growing number of schools that are developing stricter standards and more stringent enforcement of existing regulations to protect their students.

Chapter 9

Sex After Termination: The Nature of Consensual Relations, the Residue of Power, and the Unresolved Issues

Earlier chapters discussed various reasons that sexual relationships between professionals and the individuals they serve can be exploitative and result in harmful and enduring consequences. This chapter considers whether, and to what extent, the same issues that create the potential for exploitation during the ongoing professional service phase of a relationship continue after that phase ends.

In some cases the professional relationship has an established course, and both parties clearly understand the beginning and the end. College professors and students, for example, both recognize from the beginning that a course, semester, or other period of academic training will, in a predictable and due course, end. A particular professor and particular student may not know whether another program will follow, but eventually the point comes when the teacher/student relationship ends. Once that phase is over, whether a subsequent intimate relationship between them is still inherently exploitative is a more problematic question.

The relationship between attorney and client, on the other hand, may or may not have an identifiable ending. For the most part, an attorney is engaged to handle a specific legal matter, and when that matter ends, the relationship terminates. There are, however, at least two exceptions to this general rule. One is when a particular legal matter may be ongoing: (1) a divorce that requires continuing supervision of the court (and hence the lawyers), or (2) a "family lawyer" relationship in which an attorney handles all of the family's legal matters as they arise from time to time. Even in those cases, however, specific legal matters are usually individual cases, and most people know that they can go elsewhere, if necessary, when the next matter arises.

The relationship between physicians and their patients is more complicated. A woman may engage her obstetrician for a limited period of time (during her childbearing years) but may retain him as her gynecologist indefinitely. Another individual may go to the same general practitioner frequently throughout her lifetime. She may consult a specialist once, or she may find that the problem recurs or another one requiring his services develops. Hence, unless there is an ongoing relationship with a regular practitioner, the physician/patient relationship is one that comes and goes without necessary or predictable regularity.

The relationship between clergy and parishioners is even more complicated. An ongoing relationship between a particular clergyman and his parishioners may be indefinite, limited only by his service to the parish. On the other hand, to the extent that a clergyman is a representative of a higher spiritual being, the relationship may continue indefinitely, even in the absence of his physical presence. Many parishioners, however, view the clergy in the same light regardless of whether they serve their parish or another. Furthermore, if the clergyman is, at some point, asked to perform pastoral counseling, his role as counselor may go through a course, with or without a defined ending, while he continues to serve the parish.

By far the most complicated relationship between professionals and their clients occurs in the mental health field. The reasons for this are many and have been discussed elsewhere in this book. They are no less complicated even after the "official" professional relationship has been terminated. In fact, the difficulty that some clients experience in terminating a therapeutic relationship reflects the effects of these complications. Because all of the concerns about sexual contact after professional services end are present in the mental health field, that discipline will be used as a benchmark, and the posttermination issues that may exist in other fields will be discussed in terms of the similarities and differences that have been noted.

MENTAL HEALTH PROFESSIONS

The question of whether sexual contact is acceptable after termination of a mental health relationship raises two issues: (1) whether it is proper to terminate the professional relationship in order to establish a personal (i.e., sexual) one and (2) whether it is proper to begin a sexual relationship after the professional relationship is terminated in due course. In all fields, the issue of sexual contact after termination calls into question the tension between wanting to protect former clients from the residual effects of the professional relationship and wanting not to interfere unduly with the freedom of individuals to enter into desired and consensual liaisons. (In the mental health field, it also raises the issue of whether the previous treatment might be "undone" if the patient is later harmed by a subsequent sexual relationship with the therapist which ends badly for the patient.)

Peggy was treated by Dr. M. for depression during a time when her daughter was suffering from leukemia. The therapy addressed many issues around the theme of separation and loss and Peggy had made significant progress in coping with the likely loss of her daughter. After the therapy ended, Peggy and Dr. M. began a sexual relationship. When inevitably it ended two-and-one-half months later, Peggy suffered even greater symptoms of depression and it appeared that she had not benefited from the therapy.

Termination often brings to the fore the personal dynamics between professional and client, some that change and others that persist even after the service is terminated.

Termination can mean different things for individuals in different contexts. Clearly it is more eventful to end a relationship with someone with whom there has been an intimate connection than with someone who has performed an isolated service which is simply no longer needed. Mental health counseling, whether in the context of psychotherapy or pastoral counseling, is certainly among the most intimate of professional relationships. That individual shares her thoughts, desires, motivations, and fantasies, exposing to another's scrutiny the most personal parts of herself. Inevitably she develops feelings about the therapist who performs that function (i.e., develops a transference). Terminating a transference relationship is an important part of the therapeutic process. It is usually accomplished through open discussion in which both parties acknowledge that a particular type of relationship has been shared. It becomes clear that this relationship arose out of and then became an important part of the treatment process. What it means to the patient to end this relationship in light of both present and past issues that are revealed through the transference is thoroughly examined. When the therapy has accomplished as much as it can, whether or not ultimate goals have been achieved, bringing it to closure (with the patient moving on to independent functioning) is a necessary part of the process.

For many patients the termination of therapy creates anxiety and apprehension. At the point of termination patients must often let go of their illusions that therapy is a cure-all, and that it will somehow transform them into different people. They usually come to understand, and even appreciate, that the therapist who seemed so powerful is human and has his limitations. The very decision to end therapy raises issues surrounding separation. Sometimes for the first time patients are forced to recognize how dependent they have become upon the therapist. Not only have they come to feel close to him, but the loss of that relationship means that they can no longer rely on the therapist's concern, understanding, and, at times, wise counsel.

> Lisa had been in therapy for almost 3 years. Her insurance, which paid for 20 weeks a year, had run out for that particular year and Lisa had come to believe that she had made as much progress as was possible. In fact, she and her therapist agreed that there had been significant gains and that she was ready to terminate. When the reality of not being able to rely on him anymore actually set in, however, Lisa experienced a deep sense of loss. They discussed this issue at their last scheduled meeting, when, to her surprise, her therapist expressed his own sorrow about losing their relationship. When he hinted that he might be interested in developing a "personal" relationship with her, Lisa felt it was an offer that was too good to pass up.

In some cases a patient may agree to (or even suggest) some other type of relationship (including a sexual one) as a way of preventing the separation. Clearly the patient's ability to evaluate the merits of a sexual relationship is clouded by her feelings of loss. Indeed, one of the important functions of the termination phase of therapy is to deal with these feelings in a constructive manner, one that helps the patient to grow out of her childhood needs and into more mature and realistic modes of relating to others.

There is considerable debate within the mental health field about whether the very nature of the therapeutic relationship and process makes sexual contact improper even after the professional phase of the relationship ends. Researchers who have studied the dynamics of this phase in order to formulate guidelines do not always agree what they should be. In fact, considerable debate continues between two points of view: some believe that a sexual relationship between therapist and former patient always "exploits" the special nature of the therapeutic relationship; others believe that after a reasonable period of time, the effects of the therapeutic relationship dissipate and individuals no longer need to be protected from their own discretionary choices.

Notwithstanding the ongoing debate, most therapists agree that even after a therapeutic relationship ends, there are residual effects of the treatment process. But do these effects subside over time, or do they ever truly end so that the therapist and patient can thereafter become involved with one another on an intimate level without "exploiting" the personal and private information revealed in the therapy? This is the subject of the ongoing debate. There is only general agreement that the factors that contribute to the unique nature of the ongoing therapeutic relationship are also those that extend the potential for exploitation beyond the termination of the therapeutic relationship.

What, exactly, are these factors? Again the most significant one is the ongoing presence of "transference," which was discussed at length in Chapter 2. Most patients develop significant transference feelings which make them vulnerable to undue influence by the therapist, upon whom the transference reactions are focused. The consequence of transference is often that the patient tends to idealize the therapist, attributing to him qualities and intentions which may, in fact, not exist. This distortion by the patient cannot be fully addressed unless a proper professional termination takes place. It is in the analysis of the transference and subsequent termination that the patient learns about her unique way of altering reality to satisfy her unfulfilled childhood needs. In so doing, she identifies more mature and realistic ways of meeting her needs. She can also see how her judgment is influenced by the transference.

At the same time, the patient's decision-making capacity may still be impaired by the very condition that brought her into the therapist's care. Individuals enter therapy for a variety of reasons, but usually there is an identifiable cause or precipitating circumstance that leads a person to seek out a psychotherapist. In addition, there are often underlying and more pervasive psychological problems which are triggered by the precipitating event. The underlying issues vary widely, of course, from patient to patient, and it is even possible that in some cases her issues do not impair her decision-making capacity at all. In a great many cases, however, the underlying psychological condition contributes significantly to the way in which the patient views her world, processes her experiences, formulates her thoughts, and directs her actions. All this can occur outside conscious thought and beyond the exercise of free will. Additionally, of course, whatever upset is associated with the precipitating circumstances contributes to her state of mind and affects her judgment.

A third element arises out of the "fiduciary" nature of the therapeutic relationship. A patient who seeks out the services of a therapist does so because she is in need of services and is willing (usually) to vest in him her trust that he will act on her behalf. Of course, the services she seeks are those which lead to a solution to the problem that brought her into therapy, not a sexual relationship. If, in response to her call for help, what she is offered is a sexual relationship, she is likely to feel that, in some way, it is the cost of receiving that help. In many cases this coercion is not understood by the patient, but instead results from the therapist's willingness to "sexualize" the relationship, that is, to allow the sexual dynamic between therapist and patient to become the focus of their relationship. The coercion usually will not take the form of an overt threat—"If you don't agree to sex, you will be abandoned." Instead, the patient is more likely to be led to believe that sex is part of her being "special" and is necessary to retain that distinction and get the benefits of his special treatment for her problem.

The theme of "abandonment" is exacerbated by another reality of the therapy: the therapist, because of the very nature of his role, has unique insight into the patient's conflicts and vulnerabilities. If his intention is to exploit that knowledge, he is likely to know when and how to do so. That knowledge of where a patient is vulnerable gives the therapist an unfair advantage in influencing or coercing a patient to consent to his wishes. This is the so-called imbalance of power that was also discussed at length in Chapter 2. The imbalance of power is no less significant where it is the patient who seeks the sexual relationship; the therapist always has the option (and, indeed, the responsibility) of working through the patient's sexual feelings without acting on them.

A final element that contributes to the possibility of exploitation is a variation on the theme that sex is somehow part of the treatment. The patient is told, or it is somehow implied, that sex with the therapist is a way of addressing and solving her problems. In fact, the role of therapist as healer is entirely inconsistent with the role of lover, and there is virtual agreement that mental health treatment cannot be provided by a sexual partner. A therapist who attempts to do both deprives the patient of the very services that he agreed to provide.

The more difficult question, of course, is how the patient is affected by these concerns after the treatment ends. One answer is that some, but not all of them dissipate when the treatment ends. For example, after termination there is no longer a concern about the therapist's performing the functions of therapist and lover at the same time, since he is no longer her therapist. Even then, however, there is the haunting question of whether the goals of therapy were met and the therapeutic relationship properly terminated if the idea of sexual involvement was being contemplated at the time.

What most authorities agree do not end, but may lessen over time, are the effects of the transference and the differences of power between the therapist and the patient. The passage of time provides the opportunity for the patient to reflect on reasons that she feels attracted to the therapist and to continue to analyze her transference reaction. It allows her to view him in a more realistic light, less distorted by the compelling feelings that are present during the therapy. Much of the debate over whether sexual contact can ever be appropriate after termination centers on the existence of residual transference. Some therapists believe that transference always remains as an overriding phenomenon; others believe that its dissipation over time eventually leaves it at a manageable level.

With respect to the inherent difference in power between the therapist and the patient, this becomes less of a factor upon the termination of therapy, particularly when patients come to realize that therapy and therefore therapists have limitations. At the same time the therapist no longer "has something," that is, his "cure" potential, which the patient needs and to which she can be held hostage. Nevertheless, some power differential continues in light of the fact that the patient's emotional vulnerabilities were the focus of the relationship. In the usual case the therapist reveals few of his own conflicts and foibles. Hence, there continues to be unequal access to one another's vulnerabilities which can still affect issues of power between them. Most practitioners agree that this subsides over time, but whether, and how soon, is a subject of ongoing debate.

> Dale formally terminated therapy about 7 months before the possibility of a sexual relationship with her prior therapist arose. He had called her a few times to see how she was doing and to "stay in touch," but for all intents and purposes the therapy had ended. During their phone conversations he always wanted to talk about her old problems, almost as though he were trying to reactivate them. In their most recent contact, Dale became very upset when she began to question her ability to attract and sustain a relationship. It was then that the therapist told her that he had always been attracted to her and asked to see her socially. Dale was overcome by this dream-come-true. She wanted to prove that she was attractive and could hold on to a man.

LAWS CONCERNING TERMINATION OF THERAPY

Because of the magnitude of this problem in the mental health professions many states have regulated therapist sexual contact with patients. Not surprisingly, in the other professions, for the most part, they have not. Even among mental health workers, however, there is disagreement about the role of the law, criminal or civil, in regulating posttermination sexual relations and many states continue to wrestle with this issue. In those states with laws making sexual behavior illegal during treatment, sexual contact after termination of the professional relationship is generally also covered. For example, California and Florida make it a criminal offense for a therapist to terminate a therapeutic relationship solely or primarily for the purpose of engaging in a sexual relationship. Thus in most cases termination of therapy in order to engage in sexual relations is viewed as if there had been an ongoing therapeutic relationship. Interestingly, however, that is not the case in California. There a therapist can avoid liability, even in those cases in which he specifically terminates a professional relationship in order to begin a sexual one, if he has referred the patient for treatment to an independent therapist. (The statute is unclear about whether the patient even has to consult the independent therapist, as long as an appropriate referral is actually made.)

Minnesota, which also regulates posttermination sex by law, is even more restrictive. Minnesota subjects a therapist to its criminal penalties if he has sexual contact with a former patient, even after treatment has been properly terminated, if, in the eyes of the court, the patient is found to have remained "emotionally dependent" on the therapist. This apparently means that at any time after the termination of a therapeutic relationship, a therapist can be found guilty of sexual misconduct if it can be proved that the patient was still emotionally dependent on him. On that basis, it would seem that he could never know, ahead of time, whether a sexual relationship with a former patient might someday subject him to criminal responsibility. In practice, however, this offense has not yet been successfully presented. If put to a serious challenge, it may also be found to be unconstitutional.

Minnesota's criminal law, like the "common law" of most states, also provides for criminal penalties if "therapeutic deception" was associated with the sexual relationship. This means that if, for example, the therapist told the patient that sexual contact was somehow part of the treatment, he would be guilty under that provision of the criminal law. In a civil court a therapist who deceives a patient in this way may be sued for fraud or a similar offense, in addition to his responsibility for sexual misconduct.

The states that impose criminal laws to regulate sexual relationships after termination of therapy usually require that there be a "waiting period" between the time that the therapeutic treatment ends and a sexual relationship begins. In most cases the waiting period is either 1 or 2 years. Not coincidentally the civil laws that exist in four states (imposing civil liability on therapists who have sex with their patients) also impose a waiting period after termination of treatment during which sexual contact is forbidden. A final provision, which some states believe is too far-reaching, is that during the "waiting period" before a sexual relationship will be permitted, the parties may not even have social contact. This mandate is difficult to regulate, and some believe it to be unnecessarily restrictive.

The professional societies which, to a greater or lesser extent, also regulate the conduct of their members have all imposed specific guidelines concerning sexual relationships with patients. To date, however, only a few have issued guidelines concerning sexual contact with former patients. They also have limited effect since no practitioner has to be a member of any professional society in order to practice his profession. Further, the most that such a society can do is to expel the individual from its membership. Neverless, these professional societies are highly influential, not only within the professions, but also with respect to the subsequent actions of regulatory (licensing) boards. Therefore, if a member is disciplined by his own professional society for conduct which violates its code of ethics, that action may influence a licensing board that gives the next ruling on the case.

OTHER PROFESSIONS

To what extent are patients, clients, or students of other professionals affected by the residual effects of the original relationship once that previous relationship has concluded? Just as in the mental health professions, the answers seem to lie with the issue of whether, and to what extent, a transference or transferencelike occurrence was a part of the relationship and whether it is likely to continue after the professional services end. In some instances a continued imbalance of power may also play a role after termination.

In Chapter 3 we discussed the transferencelike issues that can occur in the attorney/client relationship (particularly in the divorce context) and described how they can affect an ongoing relationship. Does a client continue to be affected by these issues after the professional relationship ends? Currently no state attempts to regulate sexual contact after termination although commentators have argued that a waiting period is in order. The argument is that even when the client's legal business is fully concluded, the transferencelike reactions, if they occurred, would take time to diminish. The power differential can also continue to be an issue, particularly with clients who may not have access to other lawyers or may not realize that they can terminate their relationship with one and engage another. In some instances (e.g., divorce and child custody cases) a client may be concerned that future disputes would best be handled by the lawyer who has been involved in her case, and thus feel dependent and not realize that she can always go to another lawyer. This puts the former client at risk for being manipulated, intimidated, and exploited.

The Code of Ethics of the American Medical Association makes it improper for a physician to enter into a relationship with a former patient in which he "uses or exploits trust, knowledge, emotions or influence derived from the previous relationship." In general medicine, unlike the position taken by the American Psychiatric Association, there is no presumption that the original relationship inherently gives rise to the potential for such exploitation. Once again, at issue is whether a power differential or transferencelike phenomenon continues after the termination of treatment. For physicians and for attorneys, and for many of the same reasons, the dynamics of transference and power do exist but probably also diminish over time. As discussed previously, some specialties such as obstetrics and gynecology are more conducive to transference reactions and more time may be required before their effect on the decision-making process diminishes.

There are no laws that attempt to regulate nonpsychiatric physicians' sexual relationships with patients after the termination of treatment. This poses an interesting irony within the mental health field in states such as Florida: psychologists, who are regulated by the Board of Psychological Examiners, are subject indefinitely to civil and even criminal penalties for sexual contact after termination, whereas psychiatrists are regulated by the medical board, which allows sexual contact immediately after termination.

Sexual contact between teachers and students after termination of an academic program is not regulated even by those colleges and universities that make it unethical while the teacher/student relationship exists.

Finally, sexual contact between clergy and former parishioners is generally not regulated, except to the extent that the clergyman performs the services of pastoral counselor. In the latter case, the clergy is subject to the same legal and ethical constraints as other mental health professionals. Notwithstanding the absence of regulations, however, sexual contact between a former clergyman and a former parishioner is likely to raise virtually the same issues that were present during his service. Even more so than for mental health workers, the unequal "power" issues remain intact.

In summary, while virtually all mental health (and counseling) professionals agree that transference and unequal power issues extend beyond the actual treatment relationship, they are not all in agreement as to the duration and severity of the effects. There continues to be a tension between a great concern for individuals who might be unwittingly exploited and a desire to allow individuals to relate to one another voluntarily, free of governmental and other institutional interference. In the absence of valid and reliable scientific data that document the harmful effects of posttermination sexual relationships, it has been difficult to impose a "per se" rule. Instead, the trend seems to be toward a "cooling off" period in which each partner takes time, after termination, to reflect on, assess, and decide whether a sexual relationship is desirable.

In all other professions where issues of transference and power are not conceptualized as being intrinsic to the professional/client relationship, and where there is even less scientific basis for regulating behavior, there are few prohibitions against individuals who choose to have an intimate relationship that develops out of the previous professional relationship. Freedom to choose one's associates is a fundamental personal right, and, at this point, there is insufficient reliable indication that former patients, clients, students, and others cannot make their own informed choices. On the other hand, the problem of sexual abuse by professionals is one that has burgeoned as an increasing number are found to be abusing their positions of trust. As research continues, the balance may shift from promoting rights of association to protecting individuals who are at risk for harmful consequences associated with sexual exploitation.

Afterword

In this volume the authors have examined the problem of sexual exploitation in professional relationships. It is clearly a complex and troubling issue, often swept under the rug out of sight. In the absence of sound scientific data, we are left to speculate about how widespread the problem really is and how profound are its effects. The authors have attempted, within the limits of present knowledge, to portray the various conditions that lead to this type of misconduct and its psychological and legal implications. What continues to be impressive is the seeming lack of professional interest in this area, at least until very recently. While mental health professionals have been pioneers in this field, others have been slow to respond. The legal profession seems to be proceeding cautiously, more likely in an effort to protect itself than out of any concern for the public welfare. The medical professions have proscribed sexual misconduct with patients since the days of the Hippocratic Oath, but only recently is it thinking earnestly about enforcing its own code. Clergy, teachers, and allied health professionals are also just beginning to acknowledge the seriousness of the problem within their ranks.

Acknowledging the problem is one thing; doing something about it is quite another. The mental health professions have acknowledged the problem for years, but they, too, have proceeded cautiously in policing their own. But slowly and surely, there is a growing effort to study the problem, document its prevalence, and develop strategies for assisting its victims. Currently professional associations are mounting widespread efforts to establish strict ethical policy and encourage legislative controls. Yet even today it is unclear exactly what direction social policy will ultimately take. While the professions struggle to confront the issue, they cannot help but be influenced by their defensive self-interest and "old boy" protectionism.

It is disheartening to those of us who see the devastating effects of sexual exploitation to witness how it can be trivialized by arguably our most influential force: Hollywood. Film makers produce and distribute powerful images and messages that confuse the issues and, more significantly, may actually desensitize the public to the seriousness of the problem by appearing to condone some clearly unethical and exploitative behavior. For example, in the 1991 Hollywood blockbuster *The Prince of Tides,* Barbra Streisand played a glamorous psychiatrist and Nick Nolte the troubled brother of her psychotic patient. Less than a year later another highly promoted film, *Final Analysis,* was released. In this popular film Richard Gere played a handsome psychiatrist and Kim Basinger the beautiful sister of his severely neurotic patient. What these widely viewed films have in common is the theme of the well-intentioned psychiatrist who becomes sexually involved with a patient's sibling. The relationship is initiated innocently, of course, to gain information that might be helpful in the treatment of the "patient." In *The Prince of Tides* the psychiatrist is involved in her own bad marriage; in *Final Analysis* the psychiatrist is simply overcome by the woman's beauty and her own abusive marriage. Granted, in neither case does the psychiatrist become involved with the identified "patient." Nevertheless it is clear in both films that the psychiatrist has extended the treatment relationship to include the sibling and, in so doing, has developed an intense relationship that can only be understood within the context of transference/countertransference phenomena. While the objects of the psychiatrists' attraction are not the patients, per se, it is undisputed that the sibling is an extension of the patient and just as deeply involved in the treatment.

In *The Prince of Tides,* the relationship is highly romanticized and there is virtually no attempt even to question the ethics of the sexual relationship. In *Final Analysis* there is a perfunctory questioning of the psychiatrist's behavior by a concerned colleague and longtime friend, but once the colleague sees how beautiful the woman is, he seems to understand the attraction and no longer questions the relationship. What is the message to the viewing public (and recipients of such services)? Could it be that such relationships are understandable and, indeed, acceptable, as long as there is adequate justification, for example, the glamour of a Hollywood sex object? What is the effect of repeated exposure to such images and messages? Could it desensitize the viewer to the unacceptable nature of such behavior and the great damage that it ultimately causes?

We are left with a classic case of a culture at odds with itself. Is this type of behavior sexually exploitative and unacceptable, or does it somehow become acceptable under the right circumstances? Does a powerful sexual attraction, a so-called affair of the heart, somehow excuse irresponsible behavior? On the one hand, a growing number of states are going so far as to declare that such relationships are criminal; on the other, Hollywood is condoning, if not glamorizing, such behavior. These mixed messages are certain at least to perpetuate the confusion, if not to dilute the efforts of those who are genuinely concerned about the problem of sexual exploitation and the betrayal of trust.

Bibliography

American Association of Sex Educators, Counselors and Therapists: Code of Ethics. Washington, D.C., 1979.

American Bar Association/Bureau of National Affairs Lawyers' Manual of Professional Conduct. Vol. 3: Current Reports. Washington, D.C., American Bar Association, 1987.

American Psychiatric Association: Diagnostic and Statistical Manual of Mental Disorders (Third Edition—Revised). Washington, D.C., 1987

American Psychiatric Association: Principles of Medical Ethics with Annotations Especially Applicable to Psychiatry. Washington, D.C., 1985.

American Psychological Association: Ethical Principles of Psychologists. Am. Psychol. 36:633–638, 1981.

American Psychological Association: If Sex Enters into the Psychotherapy Relationship. Washington, D.C., 1987.

Barbara A. v. John G., 145 Cal. App. 3d. 369 (1983).

Bates, C. M., Brodsky, A. M.: Sex in the Therapy Hour: A Case of Professional Incest. New York, Guilford Press, 1989.

Borenzweig, H.: Touching in Clinical Social Work. Social Casework 64:238–242, 1983.

Burgess, A. W.: Physician Sexual Misconduct and Patients' Responsibilities. Am. J. Psychiatry 138:1335–1342, 1981.

Burgess, A. W., Hartman, C. R.: Sexual Exploitation of Patients by Health Professionals. New York, Praeger, 1986.

Collins, D. T., Mebed, A. K., Mortimer, R. L.: Patient-Therapist Sex: Consequences for Subsequent Treatment. McLean Hosp. J. 3(1):24–36, 1978.

Cotton v. Kambly, 300 N.W.2d 627 (Mich Ct. App. 1980).

Destafano v. Grabian, 763 P.2d 275 (Colo. 1988).

Dyer, A. R.: Ethics and Psychiatry. Washington D.C., American Psychiatric Press, 1988.

Dziech, B., Weiner, L.: The Lecherous Professor: Sexual Harassment on Campus. Boston, Beacon Press, 1984.

Edelwich, J.: Sexual Dilemmas for the Helping Professions. New York, Brunner/Mazel, 1982.

Feldman-Summers, S., Jones, G.: Psychological Impacts of Sexual Contact Between Therapists or Other Health Care Practitioners and Their Clients. J. Consult. Clin. Psychol. 52:1054–1061, 1984.

Fortune, M. M.: Is Nothing Sacred? When Sex Invades the Pastoral Relationship. San Francisco, Harper & Row, 1989.

Freeman, L., Roy, J.: Betrayal: The True Story of the First Woman to Successfully Sue Her Psychiatrist for Using Sex in the Guise of Therapy. New York: Stein and Day, 1976.

Freud, S.: Observations on Transference Love (1915). In Complete Psychological Works, standard edition, vol. 12. Translated and edited by Strachey, J. London, Hogarth Press, 1958.

Gobbard, C.O., ed.: Sexual Exploitation in Professional Relationships. Washington, D.C., American Psychiatric Press, 1989.

Gartrell, N., Herman, J., Olarte, S., et al.: Psychiatrist-Patient Sexual Contact: Results of a National Survey. Am. J. Psychiatry 143:112–131, 1986.

Glater, R. D., Thorpe, J. S.: Unethical Intimacy: A Survey of Sexual Contact and Advances Between Psychology Educators and Female Graduate Students. Am. Psychol. 41:43–51, 1986.

Hartlaub, G. H., Martin, G. C., Rhine, M. W.: Recontact with the Analyst Following Termination: A Survey of 71 Cases. J. Am. Psychoanal. Assoc. 34:895–910, 1986.

Herman, J. L., Gartrell, N., Olarte, S., et al. Psychiatrist-Patient Sexual Contact: Results of a National Survey. II: Psychiatrists' Attitudes. Am. J. Psychiatry 144:164–169, 1987.

Holroyd, J. C., Brodsky, A. M.: Psychologists' Attitudes and Practices Regarding Erotic and Neurotic Physical Contact with Patients. Am. Psychol. 32:843–849, 1977.

Holtzman, B. L.: Who's The Therapist Here: Dynamics Underlying Therapist-Client Sexual Relations. Smith College Studies in Social Work 54:204–224, 1984.

In re Marriage of Kanter, 581 N.E.2d 6 (Ill. App. 1991).

Keith Spiegel, P., Koocher, G.: Ethics in Psychology: Professional Standards and Cases. Hillsdale, N.J., Lawrence Erlbaum Press, 1985.

Morin v Drucker, No. C-90-590 (Belknap Cty. Super. Ct., Laconia, N.H. 1992).

Munich, A: Seduction in Academe. Psychology Today 82–84, 108, February 1978.

National Association of Social Workers: Code of Ethics of the National Association of Social Workers. Washington, D.C., 1980.

Nicholson v. Han, 12 Mich. App. 35, 162 N.W.2d 313 (1968).

Norman H., Blacker, K., Oremland, J., et al: The Fate of the Transference Neurosis After Termination of a Satisfactory Analysis. J. Am. Psychoanal. Assoc. 24:471–498, 1976.

Noto v. St. Vincent's Hospital, 142 Misc.2d 292, 537 N.Y.S.2d 446 (1988).

Perry, J.: Physicians' Erotic and Nonerotic Physical Involvement with Patients. Am. J. Psychiatry 133:838–840, 1976.

Plasil, E.: Therapist: The Shocking Autobiography of a Woman Sexually Exploited by Her Analyst. New York, St. Martins/Marck, 1985.

Pope, K. S.: Research and Laws Regarding Therapist-Patient Sexual Involvement: Implications for Therapists. Am. J. Psychother. 40:564–571 1986a.

Pope, K. S., Bouhoutsos, J.: Sexual Intimacy Between Therapists and Patients. New York, Praeger, 1986.

Pope, K. S., Keith-Spiegel, P., Tabachnick, B. G.: Sexual Attraction to Clients: The Human Therapist and the (Sometimes) Inhuman Training System. Am. Psychol. 41:147–158, 1986.

Pope, K. S., Levenson H., Schoer, L. R.: Sexual Intimacy in Psychology Training: Results and Implications of a National Survey. Am. Psychol. 34:682–689, 1979.

Rassieur, C.: The Problem Clergymen Don't Talk About. Philadelphia, Westminster Press, 1976.

Recent Ethics Cases. Psychiatr. News 17(8):8–9, 38, April 1982.

Riley v. Presnell, 409 Mass. 239 (1991).

Roy v. Hartogs, 381 N.Y.S.2d 587 (1976).

St. Paul Fire & Marine Ins. Co. v. Vigilant Ins. Co., 919 F.2d 235 (4th Cir. 1990).

Saul, L. J.: The Erotic Transference. Psychoanal. Q. 31:54–61, 1962.

Schoener, G., Migrover, J., Gonsiorek, J.: Responding Therapeutically to Clients Who Have Been Sexually Involved with Their Psychotherapists. Minneapolis, Monographs, Walk-In Counseling Center, 1981.

Searles, H. F.: Countertransference and Related Subjects. New York, International University Press, 1979.

Sell, J. M., Gottlieb, M. C., Shoenfeld, L.: Ethical Considerations of Social/Romantic Relationships with Present and Former Clients. Prof. Psychology Res. Pract. 17:504–508, 1986.

Simmons v. United States, 805 F.2d 1363 (9th Cir. 1986).

Simon, R.: The Psychiatrist as a Fiduciary: Avoiding the Double-Agent Rule. Psychiatr. Ann. 17:622–626, 1987.

Smith, J. T., Bisbing, S. B.: Sexual Exploitation by Professionals. Potomac, Md., Legal Medicine Press, 1986

Sonne, J., Meyer, C. B., Borys D., et al: Clients' Reactions to Sexual Intimacy in Therapy. Am. J. Orthopsychiatry 55:183–189, 1985.

Stone, A. A.: The Legal Implications of Sexual Activity Between Psychiatrist and Patient. Am. J. Psychiatry 133:1138–1141, 1976.

Stone, A. A.: Law, Psychiatry and Morality. Washington, D.C., American Psychiatric Press, 1984.

Suppressed v. Suppressed, 206 Ill. App. 3d. 918, 565 N.E.2d 101 (1990).

Taylor, B., Wagner, N.: Sex Between Therapists and Clients: A Review and Analysis. Prof. Psychology 7:593–601, 1976.

Tenner, D.: Love and Limerence: The Experience of Being in Love. New York, Stein and Day, 1979.

Walker, E., Young, P. D.: A Killing Cure. New York, Holt, Rinehart & Winston, 1988.

Webb, W.: The Doctor-Patient Covenant and the Threat of Exploitation. Am. J. Psychia-
    try 143:1149–1150, 1986.
Whitfield, C. W.: Boundaries and Relationships: Knowing, Protecting and Enjoying the
    Self. Deerfield Beach, Fla., Health Communications, 1993.
Zipkin v. Freeman, 436 S.W.2d 753 (Mo. 1968).

Index

About the Authors

JOEL FRIEDMAN is a psychologist who has served for the past 20 years on the faculty of the Harvard Medical School and the Massachusetts General Hospital. He is the co-author of *Women and the Law, Law and Gender Bias, Sexual Harassment,* and *Date Rape.*

MARCIA MOBILIA BOUMIL is a faculty member of Tufts University School of Medicine. She is the author of numerous articles and the co-author of *Medical Liability, Women and the Law, Law and Gender Bias, Sexual Harassment, Date Rape,* and *Law, Ethics and Reproductive Choice.*